Understanding G4

The Concise Guide to Next Generation Sustainability Reporting

Elaine Cohen

Founder and CEO, Beyond Business Ltd

tw: @elainecohen

e: info@b-yond.biz

w: www.b-yond.biz

bl: www.csr-reporting.blogspot.com

bl: www.csrforhr.com

bl: www.csr-books.com

Author of:

- *CSR for HR: A Necessary Partnership for Advancing Responsible Business Practices* (Greenleaf, 2010)

- *Sustainability Reporting for SMEs Competitive Advantage through Transparency* (Dō Sustainability, 2013)

First published in 2013 by Dō Sustainability

87 Lonsdale Road, Oxford OX2 7ET, UK

ISBN 978-1-909293-64-9 (eBook-ePub)

ISBN 978-1-909293-65-6 (eBook-PDF)

ISBN 978-1-909293-63-2 (Paperback)

A catalogue record for this title is available from the British Library.

Dō Sustainability strives for net positive social and environmental impact. See our sustainability policy at **www.dosustainability.com**.

Page design and typesetting by Alison Rayner

Cover by Becky Chilcott

For further information on Dō Sustainability, visit our website: **www.dosustainability.com**

DōShorts

Dō **Sustainability** is the publisher of **DōShorts**: short, high-value ebooks that distil sustainability best practice and business insights for busy, results-driven professionals. Each DōShort can be read in 90 minutes.

New and forthcoming DōShorts – stay up to date

We publish 3 to 5 new DōShorts each month. The best way to keep up to date? Sign up to our short, monthly newsletter. Go to **www. dosustainability.com/newsletter** to sign up to the Dō Newsletter. Some of our latest and forthcoming titles include:

- *How to Account for Sustainability: A Business Guide to Measuring and Managing* Laura Musikanski
- *Sustainability in the Public Sector: An Essential Briefing for Stakeholders* Sonja Powell
- *Sustainability Reporting for SMEs: Competitive Advantage Through Transparency* Elaine Cohen
- *REDD+ and Business Sustainability: A Guide to Reversing Deforestation for Forward Thinking Companies* Brian McFarland
- *How Gamification Can Help Your Business Engage in Sustainability* Paula Owen
- *Sustainable Energy Options for Business* Philip Wolfe
- *Adapting to Climate Change: 2.0 Enterprise Risk Management* Mark Trexler & Laura Kosloff
- *Sustainable Transport Fuels Business Briefing* David Thorpe
- *How to Engage Youth to Drive Corporate Responsbility: Roles and Interventions* Nicolò Wojewoda

- *The Short Guide to Sustainable Investing*   Cary Krosinsky

- *Strategic Sustainability: Why it Matters to Your Business and How to Make it Happen*   Alexandra McKay

- *Sustainability Decoded: How to Unlock Profit Through the Value Chain*   Laura Musikanski

- *Working Collaboratively: A Practical Guide to Achieving More* Penny Walker

Subscriptions

In addition to individual sales of our ebooks, we now offer subscriptions. Access 60+ ebooks for the price of 5 with a personal subscription to our full e-library. Institutional subscriptions are also available for your staff or students. Visit **www.dosustainability.com/books/subscriptions** or email **veruschka@dosustainability.com**

Write for us, or suggest a DōShort

Please visit **www.dosustainability.com** for our full publishing programme. If you don't find what you need, write for us! Or suggest a DōShort on our website. We look forward to hearing from you.

....

Abstract

SUSTAINABILITY REPORTING IS HERE to stay and is expanding its influence. The launch of the Global Reporting Initiative (GRI) G4 Sustainability Reporting Framework took place in May 2013, and since then, thousands of reporters are grappling with the questions: "Should we report using the G4 framework?" "What's the significance of the changes and how do they affect our reporting?" "What is the right reporting level for our company?" "What should we do next?" "How do we decide?" GRI has published detailed guidelines in the form of two manuals, adding up to 300 pages of technical guidance, but distilling the main advantages, risks, challenges and opportunities for all different types of reporting companies is no easy task. In this book, Elaine Cohen cuts to the chase, presenting an easy-to-follow review of everything any company needs to know in order to decide whether to use the G4 Framework and if so, how. If you want to know what G4 means for corporate reporters, whether they are first-timers, SMEs, experienced global companies or existing GRI reporters at any level, this book is for you. It will give you the answers you need to make decisions, in a user-friendly format, to help you along your reporting journey. This book will also help users of reports know what to expect from the new generation of G4 sustainability reports and reporting consultants, as they advise clients on reporting process, content and disclosure.

About the Author

 **ELAINE COHEN** is passionate about CSR, HR, sustainability reporting, social justice and ice cream! Elaine is the founder and managing consultant of Beyond Business Ltd, an *inspired* CSR consulting and sustainability reporting firm, serving a long list of international companies. Prior to work in this field, Elaine gained over 20 years of business experience with Procter & Gamble (eight years in Supply Chain Executive roles in Europe), with Unilever (eight years as VP for Human Resources with Unilever Israel) and a range of other roles with smaller companies.

Elaine makes a contribution to the community as a Chair of a Women's Empowerment non-profit organization and assisting students. Elaine lectures widely on CSR, is a committed blogger on sustainability reporting via her blog (**www.csr-reporting.blogspot.com**), provides expert reviews of sustainability reports for CorporateRegister.com (**www.corporateregister. com**) and *Ethical Corporation Magazine* (**www.ethicalcorp.com**), and writes in many printed journals and websites. Elaine authored the first ever book on the interface between CSR and Human Resources (*CSR for HR*, Greenleaf, 2010) and a first on small company reporting: *Sustainability Reporting for SMEs: Competitive Advantage through Transparency* (Dō Sustainability, 2013).

Disclaimer

THIS BOOK IS NOT AN OFFICIAL PUBLICATION of the Global Reporting Initiative and its content has not been reviewed by any member of the GRI in an official capacity. This book is entirely the work of the author and based on her understanding and interpretation of GRI G4 materials in the public domain at the time of writing (June 2013). Every effort has been made by the author to present the G4 guidelines in an accurate way, as an efficient tool and guide for reporters and report-users, but it is possible that there are errors, and therefore, the author does not accept liability for errors or interpretations not intended by the Global Reporting Initiative nor for future changes to the G4 framework which may affect the guidance provided in this book.

Note

GRI's G4 Guidelines are intended for any organization that wishes to report on its sustainability performance. While there are some pioneering public agencies, NGOs and academic institutions that publish sustainability reports, and for whom G4 may be relevant, the focus of this guide is corporations, of whatever size, in whatever location. Therefore, where G4 typically refers to 'organizations', this book tends to refer to 'companies'.

All GRI publications mentioned in this book relating to the GRI G4 guidelines can be found and freely downloaded via the GRI website: **www.globalreporting.org**.

Contents

Who This Book Is For

THIS BOOK IS RELEVANT for a wide range of professionals and other stakeholders who have a professional, personal or academic interest in sustainability reporting. It will be of particular interest to those charged with delivering corporate sustainability reports, but it is also a source of useful, practical and compact information and guidance for the many different users of sustainability reports who seek to understand, quickly and efficiently, what they can expect from a company in the communication of their sustainability impacts using the GRI G4 Reporting Framework. The table below offers some guidance, for you, whoever you are, wherever you are.

You are:	This book will help you because:
A Chief Sustainability Officer, CSR Manager or other senior manager charged with delivering a corporate sustainability report	You should use this book as your G4 guide at every step of the sustainability report compilation process and even a little before that. This book distils the key information that you will need as you prepare your sustainability report, and guides you through the use of the G4 guidelines in a concise and compact way and clarifies issues of interpretation and balanced use of G4. For first-time reporters, no prior knowledge of the GRI guidelines is required, though this is helpful. For existing G3 reporters, the book includes useful tables and explanations comparing G4 to former G3, facilitating your transition to G4.

You are:	This book will help you because:
An SME owner or manager	This book makes G4 accessible to you, as a small company. It demystifies 300 pages of G4 technical guidance and turns it into workable steps, considering the specific challenges small companies face. It will help you understand the benefits of G4 reporting for your small company and give you a measure of the effort involved in compiling your first report.
A CEO, seeking to know enough about the G4 guidelines to help you direct the work of your Sustainability team	Most CEOs are not involved in the detail of sustainability reporting. This book will help you understand what your reporting team is charged with delivering, and how your report meets stakeholder needs. It will help you understand what to look for in your G4 report and know whether your team has created a piece of communication which is both appealing and aligned with global best practice. As you are a busy CEO, this book is short enough to read on a flight or a train.
A CSR or sustainability consultant supporting sustainability programs in companies and report preparation	G4 should be music to your ears. It legitimizes and emphasizes the need for process and focus on important sustainability issues. By understanding and incorporating G4 into the guidance you provide for companies, your contribution will be more meaningful and probably more impactful. Use this book to get to know what's expected of your clients and guide them through critical processes.

UNDERSTANDING G4: THE CONCISE GUIDE TO NEXT GENERATION SUSTAINABILITY REPORTING

You are:	This book will help you because:
A sustainability report writer	G4 is a dream for report writers. It provides a platform for compelling narrative about meaningful issues. It legitimizes your involvement beyond writing to ensure you understand the processes and how to reflect them appropriately in a G4 report. While your writing and compilation should align with G4 'In Accordance' requirements, the laborious detail of compiling a GRI Index and ensuring the report contains empty words in order to meet an irrelevant Disclosure on Management Approach is no longer necessary. This book is an indispensable guide as you consider report structure and essential content.
A sustainability report assurer	G4 presents new opportunities for assurers of reports to play a meaningful role in setting expectations for companies as they start their G4 report. Materiality process is the new pivotal axis on which G4 reports are written. As an assurer of a G4 report, it is inconceivable that you can assure without addressing the way companies have approached materiality. This book will help you know what is expected of G4 reporters, and therefore, what you must be prepared to assure.

You are:	This book will help you because:
An academic with an interest in sustainable business	As an academic, G4 reports are a platform for understanding key business impacts on our sustainable society and planet. G4 reports, done well, will direct you quickly to the most important issues that could be the subject of research or academic study. Further, as G4 is a significant departure from former reporting guidelines, requiring a deeper approach to sustainability and its integration into business strategy, the transition to G4 will provide a wealth of fascinating insights into how companies change. This book will guide you in what G4 requires of companies and therefore what could be appropriate for study and research.
An investor in any company	As an investor, your prime interest will probably be financial information. However, more and more, so-called 'non-financial' information is relevant to the way your investment performs, as material environment, social and governance risks and opportunities often translate into big money. G4 reports position these major sustainability issues in a way that helps you understand a company's approach to these risks and related sustainability performance. As an investor, understanding G4 reporting will help you understand the implications for your investments. Equally, if, as an investor, you have an interest in Integrated Reporting, understanding the G4 framework will guide you in what sustainability-related information to seek from an Integrated Report.

You are:	This book will help you because:
A shareholder of any company	As a shareholder of a company, you want to understand not only the ways in which a company will deliver a return on your investment, but also the risks and challenges the company faces. G4 reports make these risks and sustainability challenges top-of-mind, and enables you, as a shareholder, to determine your position. Understanding G4 is key to this. This book will help you do that, quickly and efficiently.
A supplier to any company	As a supplier to a company who uses the GRI G4 Framework to report on sustainability, this book will help you understand how your customer thinks and acts, and possibly, how the customer will expect you to think and act, as a supplier. Sooner or later, and especially with the G4 enhanced focus on supply chain, you will be required to become part of your customers' reporting process, in one way or another. Read this book to help you get prepared.
A stakeholder of any company	As a customer, employee, environmentalist, community member or member of any other stakeholder group, G4 should be of interest to you. You should look for how companies are impacting your lives and the causes you care about. You don't want to waste time wading through piles of irrelevant, incomparable data. You want to understand the meaningful ways in which companies affect you and how to engage with them. By using this book to understand how companies should report with G4, you will be able to respond appropriately and influence companies more effectively.

Why I Wrote *Understanding G4*

WHY PAY FOR A BOOK ON G4, the new Sustainability Reporting Framework launched by the Global Reporting Initiative (GRI) in May 2013, when all the materials are freely downloadable from the GRI website? Check it out. Take a minute to navigate to **www.globalreporting.org** and look for the G4 symbol on the homepage, click once, and you have immediate access to the two books which form the new G4 guidelines: the book of Reporting Principles and Standard Disclosures (94 pages) and the Implementation Manual (266 pages). Both books are downloadable, for free, as many times as you want. No password needed. In addition, there are many writers on the internet, including myself, who have published summaries of the G4 changes and what they mean for reporters. I collected at least 15 different, mostly helpful, articles and summaries, in the two weeks following the G4 launch and many more since then. This is a wealth of free advice and helpful in understanding what G4 means. So why pay? Why do you need this book and how will it help you? What value does *Understanding G4* add?

Here's the thing. Even if you decide to invest a day in wading through the report-techno-babble-speak of 360 pages of GRI guideline manuals, you still may be left a little perplexed as to how G4 will actually help you advance along your reporting journey. Maybe you already tried. You may be able to appreciate the primary technical changes, such as the fact that materiality is now center-stage and determines much of the report content, and that governance and remuneration disclosures have become impossibly detailed, but the overall value of G4 may still escape you. I'll be even a little bolder. It *will* escape you. The G4 manuals, detailed and orderly though they may be, do not help you answer the question: *when should my organization start using the G4 guidelines, and how?* This book aims to help you answer that question, and it's relevant for existing reporters and new reporters.

But that's not all. Reporting companies or aspiring reporters are not the only ones affected by the G4 guidelines. There are stakeholders. Readers of reports. Assurers of reports. Users and students of reports. What does G4 mean for all these groups? How will customers, consumers, employees, investors and financial analysts understand the G4 report? I maintain, as you will see, that G4 is quite some departure from the box-ticking, shopping-list, PR-oriented, mechanical approach most companies have taken with regard to sustainability reporting. Readers of G4 reports need to approach sustainability reporting with a different paradigm. G4 reports, done well, will be very different from G3 reports, and offer a different kind of value to stakeholders who use them. More value in many ways, less value in others. For companies, G4 helps articulate the issues that affect their sustainable success and the way in which they need to account for, and manage, these issues. For readers and users, G4 reports will facilitate an understanding of these most important issues, which represent the ways in which the activities of companies affect our lives and those of our children and grandchildren, neighbors, communities and the overall ecosystem in which we aspire to survive and thrive. In any case, G4 report users must substantively reset their expectations. This book will help G4 report users do this, and know what they should be able to expect from a G4 report, and what they should not expect.

I will not hide that my prime motivation in writing this book is to advance the rapid uptake of the G4 Sustainability Reporting Framework, by offering a simple and straightforward guide to help companies adopt or adapt, in a straightforward, no frills and no techno-babble way, while ensuring stakeholders get what they are trying to do. While there are some omissions, inadequacies and even oddities in G4, I view the new framework as a major leap forward for sustainability reporting. I believe it elevates sustainability reporting to a very serious platform which is right at the heart of the way business gets done, and holds tangible advantages for reporters and report-users, as long as all are on the same page in terms of what to expect and how to apply the G4 Framework with diligence, intelligence, integrity and a genuine desire to advance sustainable business in a sustainable society on a sustainable planet.

There's more. G4 is the future. It will have a life of at least seven years, maybe more. Now that G4 is out there, G3 is history. Who wants to report on sustainability using an anachronous framework? Doing so projects low-capacity for change, low adaptability, agility and responsiveness and this will negatively impact the G3-clingers-on during the two-year transition period. G4 is here. Companies that take the early adopter approach will be admired, and the laggers will be punished. This book is a way for me to help early adoption and show companies that, while a shift is needed, and beneficial, it is by no means an impossible leap into the darkness.

G4 has been largely positively received by the global crowd of analytical professionals who have taken time to review and pronounce on the key changes. Most recognize it as helping support our advance toward sustainable business. There has been a range of commentaries ranging from the frenetically (and in some cases, unjustly) critical to the warmly embracing, with the optimistically cautious in between. The majority of writers have addressed the technical changes of G4 versus its predecessor framework, but few have gone beyond the detail to provide a true assessment of the meaning of the changes and the outcomes they are designed to deliver for reporting organizations and report users. This book is no less about the technicalities of G4 as it is about the meaning and impact of G4. Of course, we'll cover the detail, but my main objective is to help drive the paradigm change and not the indicator-by-indicator change. This book should help drive home the how of G4 and not only the what.

As I write, I am already working on two G4 reports for clients, in my capacity as a sustainability consultant and reporter. I like it. It's clearer. It seems more meaningful. It seems like a new and refreshing challenge. I have realized that G4 helps me as a consultant to add value in the reporting process – beyond just helping companies to articulate their sustainability messages and tick the right GRI boxes, I now feel that I have a more relevant and influential role in helping companies reflect the right things as well as reflect them in the right way. I feel G4 gives me a more compelling justification to urge my clients into a process-oriented approach to sustainability management and reporting, rather than being a near passive recipient of a range of materials that need to be copy-written into a coherent message, even if there is little substance behind the stories, helping companies to smooth over the cracks and gaps. For consultants, G4 is a much more favorable platform for influence and support and improves the value we offer to our clients.

Distilling this down into my specific objectives in writing this book, which I hope will add value, there are five key points.

Understanding G4 is designed to:

- Make G4 more accessible and practical for report writers and users.

- Align expectations of G4 reports for writers and users.

- Promote a rapid, quality uptake of G4 in the context of a new reporting paradigm.

- Help reporting consultants deliver greater value to reporting companies.

- Give readers value (for money) in a form not currently available elsewhere.

This book will not avoid your needing to open and use the GRI G4 Manuals, or other reference documents, but it is my hope that it distils down all the main points into a short, easy-to-understand guide which will help both experienced and novice reporters get on the G4 road.

A few words of thanks. I am very grateful to the folks at Dō Sustainability (Nick Bellorini, Gudrun Freese and team) who offer me a fabulous platform to help advance sustainability knowledge and practice through the DōShorts series. I am also grateful to all the clients of Beyond Business Ltd around the world, who provide me with opportunities to serve them and in doing so, help me stay at the forefront of best global sustainability reporting practice. Thanks also to the GRI who has done an admirable job with G4, against all odds, and in particular, to Bastian Buck, GRI Senior Manager, Reporting Framework, who patiently spent time with me on the telephone after the G4 launch, responding to my detailed questions and providing valuable insight. Thank you to all those who have contributed comments for this book, and an especially massive thank you to Dr Glenn Frommer, Head of Corporate Sustainability, Mass Transit Railway Corporation Ltd, and a very experienced sustainability reporter, who kindly reviewed the manuscript in draft form and provided invaluable guidance, suggestions and advice. This book is significantly better as a result of Glenn's input. More thanks to Rowland Hill, Sustainability and Reporting Manager at Marks & Spencer, one of the most experienced sustainability reporters around who consistently delivers winning reports which are among the most widely read, and deservedly so. Rowland kindly agreed to provide the foreword for this book and I am grateful for the UK train service which afforded him a few hours to read the manuscript and pen some excellent insights. Thanks also to Iris Rakovitzky of Beyond Business Ltd, who also reviewed the manuscript and discovered many of my typing errors, now, thankfully, corrected. Thank you to all those who have written about G4, to all those I met and engaged with at the GRI conference in Amsterdam in May 2013 – you have all helped me crystallize my own position, and write this book, in many ways.

Thank you for reading this short guide to G4. I hope you find it useful. Please don't hesitate to contact me at **info@b-yond.biz** with your thoughts and feedback. If this book helps you with your G4 reporting, please do let me know. I would love to share your experiences on my blog!

And a dedication. I cannot write another book without dedicating it, again, to my children, Eden and Amit Cohen, now aged 15 and 11, who love seeing their name in print... again and again!

Elaine Cohen
June 2013

Foreword

by Rowland Hill

Sustainability and Reporting Manager, Marks & Spencer

THIS FOURTH GENERATION of the Global Reporting Initiative (GRI) is arguably the most important since the launch of the first version back in 2000. The first GRI came into a world where progressive companies had just come to terms with environmental reporting and were looking for the next step. At the same time, many stakeholders with an interest in corporate impacts were looking for ways to improve transparency and GRI provided both – complete with a United Nations stamp of quality. There were few critical expectations and it filled the void admirably. But times have changed.

There's no doubting the impact that GRI has had on corporate reporting. It is by far the most commonly used non-financial reporting framework and has been adopted as the basis of benchmark calculations by most of the major ethical investment indices. Yet over a decade on, big questions still remain unanswered, starting with who these reports are intended for? It's not the aforementioned ethical benchmarks who prefer their data in spreadsheet form, nor is it the stakeholders who crave corporate engagement rather than reading about it. A current line of thought is that by lifting the whole of GRI into an annual financial report the value of the content will be transformed and will gain a new more influential audience. The non-financial content of Annual Reports certainly needs to be improved but in my view, it's questionable whether this combining of data can create a single audience. This year, at M&S we've taken the step of including an operational environmental, a workforce relationship and a product sustainability measurement as 'high level' key performance indicators in our Annual Report and Plan A (Sustainability) Report.

Then there's all the data! Some is just that – a measurement of an impact. Some is a forecast of where it will end up. Very little is directed by clear management ambition and a target. When we launched our Plan A sustainability program we were very clear that it had to fulfill the purpose of improving our performance, so with few exceptions, all data was subject to a target. If we didn't feel that it needed to be improved, what's the point of publishing it?

Then the vexed question of materiality, or what to include. Being all things to all men has been both a strength and weakness of GRI. How do you define materiality and the issues that should be reported on? It's easy to add to the list but difficult to edit. All activities have an impact on someone. So does that make all impacts material to all companies? What if it's a little impact that is then subject to a big media campaign – does that make it material? A big brand can be leveraged by pressure groups (and governments) in order to illustrate a concern, so do bigger brands have a greater number of material impacts simply because they carry greater expectations? There's no easy answer but when we consulted to develop Plan A we found that GRI missed 80% of the content that our stakeholders felt relevant for a UK retailer, issues such as sustainable raw materials, measuring product environmental footprints and community campaigns. Finally, consider that virtually all the large global companies caught up in the various crisis of confidence in recent years have been publishing high quality GRI reports right up to the point where it all went wrong, and often with the key data being transparently reported within huge volumes of 'other stuff'.

So, unlike in 2000, when the grateful world accepted what it was given, the fourth generation has questions to answer. Clearly the good folks of GRI have worked hard to address what they could, but challenges still remain. Has it overstepped the mark and become too complex and unwieldy?

This publication will help you to understand G4, but this time around, the future of GRI will also be shaped by other factors such as increased national regulation (on reporting) and the development of Integrated Reports.

Rowland Hill
June 2013

....

CHAPTER 1

Why GRI and Why G4?

WHEN STARTING OR CONTINUING on the reporting journey, with every new sustainability report, each company has a choice: GRI-based or not GRI-based. While this book is not really about whether or not to use the GRI framework, but rather, how to use the new G4 framework, it seems appropriate to consider, given the major change from G3 to G4, whether G4 is actually still relevant and if GRI should continue to be the obvious choice for reporters. These are my thoughts.

Why GRI? Why not just do your own thing? Or use another framework?

Why even consider a GRI-based report? Why not just report in your own way, or use another type of framework (although there is none as detailed and all-encompassing as the GRI Framework). The GRI even offers its own ready-made G4 get-out clause to enable you to have your cake and eat it – if you use the guidelines, but are not ready to be 'in accordance', then you can include the sentence: 'This report contains Standard Disclosures from the GRI Sustainability Reporting Guidelines' (G4IM, p. 50).

My view is that GRI is the leading and highly respected de facto global standard for sustainability reporting, and as such, reflects the leadership and relative engagement of the companies that use it. The GRI Framework sets a standard which is indicative of a collaborative, rather than an insular, mindset. It was developed with the expertise of a large range of highly qualified professionals from different fields and creates the promise of relevant and quality reporting, providing a thorough, reputationally positive platform for your sustainability report. GRI enables you not to reinvent the wheel, but to utilize the cumulative articulation of general stakeholder expectations around sustainability. To me, GRI-based reporting seems to be the only sensible choice for serious sustainability reporters. G4, then, is now the way to go.

However, the advantage of the GRI is only realized when the framework is applied with rigor. Not being a certifiable standard, the door is wide open for misuse, or abuse, of the guidelines. Current reports range from demonstrating the highest degree of adherence to sloppy, inaccurate and in some cases, entirely misleading or even deceitful use of the guidelines. If you are planning to use G4, and deliver an 'in accordance'

Abbreviations used in references to GRI published documents and G4 content:

- **RPSD**: Reporting Principles and Standard Disclosures booklet (Book 1 of the GRI G4 Framework)
- **G4IM**: G4 Implementation Manual
- **GSD**: General Standard Disclosure
- **SSD**: Specific Standard Disclosure
- **DMA**: Disclosure on Management Approach

G4 disclosures are referred to as G4-X, where X is the number of the relevant disclosure, as listed in the GRI published materials.

---

report at whatever level, my plea is: do it right. Don't wing it. Take it seriously. Report with integrity. Business sustainability and the reporting movement are not helped by sloppy reporting. If you are going to be sloppy, or untruthful, then don't use the GRI framework.

Overall, G4 has good points and less good points, and offers some opportunities. See Figure 1.

. . . .

FIGURE 1. The G4 SWOT.

The G4 SWOT

STRENGTHS	WEAKNESSES
• Global exposure and credibility as a new sustainability reporting framework, backed by a large body of high-profile supporters. • New focus on materiality regarded as highly relevant. • Places ownership on companies to select what is most important to disclose with respect to stakeholder interest and business impacts, rather than prescribing content. • Aligns (to some extent) with other leading sustainability platforms such as CDP, UNGC, OECD. • Value chain approach for Material Aspect Boundaries encourages companies to look beyond direct impacts. • Clear and logical format, easy to work with.	• Individual selection of material issues and possibility of narrow aspect boundary focus, in the absence of a defined set of basic indicators, makes comparability virtually impossible in G4 reports. • Assurance remains a low priority within G4 and recognition for assurance is not actively supported. • Materiality guidance is not rigorous- and may result in wide variations of number, type and range of material issues, making it almost impossible for realistic evaluation of relevance. • CORE and COMPREHENSIVE options are miles apart, making it difficult for companies to demonstrate gradual progress in sustainability transparency.

OPPORTUNITIES	THREATS
• G4 based reporting provides an opportunity for companies to enhance their value, as well as derive greater value from the reporting process. • G4-based reports could help drive more relevant and aligned reporting within industry sectors. • CORE level reporting provides an accessible entry to sustainability reporting for first time and SME reporters. • Materiality focus could be more appealing to investors and financial analysts. • Focused content may help engage broader stakeholder interest on higher impact issues which are truly relevant.	• New approaches such as SASB and individual sector initiatives, together with an attraction of Integrated Reporting, may present a short-cut for companies to meet the needs of (mainly financial) stakeholders and stop producing broader G4-type Sustainability Reports. • COMPREHENSIVE reporting will be seen as too stretching and will not be adopted, undermining the value of G4. • Sloppy use of G4 may undermine G4's credibility as a reporting framework. • Stakeholder dormancy may prevail, leaving companies unchecked in how they apply G4.

. . . .

Time will tell as to whether the threats will turn out to be real problems for uptake of the G4 Framework. The option to cherry-pick G4 and refer to the guidelines without declaring a CORE or COMPREHENSIVE level may be tempting to many, possibly because companies will judge that some of the very detailed GSDs are of little relevance and importance to stakeholders, despite GRI's due process in developing G4. I believe that there will be great benefits – and opportunities – for all if G4 is widely accepted, as you probably have realized. Therefore GRI should have a vested interest in encouraging more and better sector guidance, improved reporting quality and enhanced stakeholder interest, as well as keeping a finger on the pulse of the viability of G4 COMPREHENSIVE, with the possibility of adding a little flex to the GSD disclosure requirements.

Bottom line

If I had to venture an opinion, it seems to me that first-time reporters, SMEs, privately owned companies and minimalist G3 B level reporters may find CORE the better option. Large MNEs, experienced A level reporters and globally publicly traded companies, especially ones which operate in jurisdictions where sustainability reporting is mandated, or those that have large and complex businesses with a high number of significant material issues, may find that COMPREHENSIVE is the only way to go, if they want to remain GRI reporters.

CHAPTER 2

What Does a G4 Report Look Like?

BEFORE WE GET INTO THE WHYS and wherefores of what G4 and how G4, and differences from G3, let's get to know the animal. When you have a G4 report in your hands, or on your desktop screen, or even via an app on your iPad, *how will you recognize it as G4?* Read on to discover five things that should give the game away.

First, the reporting company should tell you it's a G4 report. The report should clearly state: 'This report has been prepared in accordance with the Global Reporting Initiative G4 guidelines' (RPSD, p. 14) *and* the report must contain a GRI Content Index (G4IM, GSD, G4-32, p. 36).

Second, the reporting company should disclose how it has applied the G4 Framework using one of two options: CORE or COMPREHENSIVE (G4IM, GSD, G4-32, p. 36).

Third, the material issues should hit you in the face. If, when you pick up a G4 report, you cannot identify the material issues within five seconds, it's not G4. Material issues should be prominently placed and quickly accessible to G4 report users.

So far, so good. This is enough to know if a report claims to be the genuine G4 item. G4 thus becomes shorthand for the content you can now reasonably expect to find in the G4 report, which is shown in Figure 2.

FIGURE 2. G4 required reporting elements.

G4 – in accordance - required reporting elements

CORE	COMPREHENSIVE
34 (of a total of 58 available) General Standard Disclosures	58 (of a total of 58 available) General Standard Disclosures
Disclosure on Management Approach for selected Material Aspects and Topics	Disclosure on Management Approach for selected Material Aspects and Topics
ONE Performance Indicator per Material Aspect or Topic, including Sector Supplement disclosures and indicators where applicable	ALL Performance Indicators per Material Aspect or Topic, including Sector Supplement disclosures and indicators where applicable

As you can see, there are two main differences between the CORE and the COMPREHENSIVE options. The first is at the level of General Standard Disclosures (GSD). COMPREHENSIVE reporters must respond to all GSDs, whereas CORE reporters can pass in three areas:

- One strategy-related GSD (G4-2: description of key impacts, risks and opportunities);

- All but one of the 22 GSDs on Governance and Remuneration. At COMPREHENSIVE level, Governance and Remuneration disclosures are far more detailed than G3 ever was, and include a host of reporting detail on governance structure, performance, role in risk management and transparency (G4-35 to G4-50), and remuneration and incentives (G51–G-55).

- Two out of three GSDs relating to ethics and integrity (G4-57 and G4-58, mechanisms for reporting ethical breaches).

The second difference is at the level of Specific Standard Disclosures. CORE reporters can opt to report against only one performance indicator per selected material topic, whereas COMPREHENSIVE reporters must go the whole way and report on every listed indicator, as well as all the additional disclosures and indicators contained in any finalized GRI Sector Supplements.

Fourth, the G4 report will contain much detail about the process of developing the selected material content (G4-18) than was required by G3, as well as a list of most material issues (G4-19). Some pre-G4 reports have included the list of prioritized material issues (commonly referred to as a Materiality Matrix) but this has been far from common practice. The strong material focus should be recognizable in any G4 report you select.

Fifth, the G4 report will contain more information about the core issues selected to report on, not only how they were selected, but why they were selected, what is so important and what the company is doing to address them. This is the elevated relevance of the Disclosure on Management Approach (DMA), which was largely under-reported in G3 (G4-DMA).

These five characteristics will make your G4 report stand out from the previous generation. In the remaining pages of this book, we will explain how to tailor your report content in alignment with these five characteristics, and also respond to the Specific Standard Disclosures (SSDs).

What does this mean?

For those of you who knew the G3 Framework, you will remember the A,B,C classification that was intended to provide a graduated entry into sustainability reporting via low transparency (Application Level C), medium transparency (Application Level B) and high transparency (Application Level A), all of which could be supplemented with a '+' to signify external assurance. This system was problematic, leading to an embarrassing and ultimately misleading culture of box-ticking and a race to include more indicators so that a company could claim higher transparency and publish self-congratulatory press releases about how great their reporting is. G4 now abolishes the A,B,C system, leaving two options only, for those reporters who wish to remain in accordance with the GRI guidelines. CORE, which may result in reports that are even less transparent than the former Application Level C, and COMPREHENSIVE which may result in reports which are even more stretching than the former Application Level A. This is potentially great news for first-time reporters and SME reporters, who now have an arguably easier way into GRI Reporting, provided they do the work. It's possibly difficult for A reporters who will be challenged by the additional disclosures in G4, but for whom the stretch is manageable.

The big question is how B level reporters will react. Should they 'demote' themselves to the lower level and move to CORE? Or should they stretch themselves way beyond historical limits and try for COMPREHENSIVE? The answer will probably lie in the quality of B reports. At GSD level, both former A and B level reporters face the same challenge of more extensive GSDs. In G4, there are 58 GSDs, versus 42 in G3 which both A and B reporters had to address. Figure 3 shows a table of the GSDs and how they compare to the G3 requirements.

In the area of Specific Standard Disclosures (performance indicators) some B level reporters have tended to stay at the minimum 20 indicators required, while others have reported far more extensively. It's possible that the high transparency Bs will make the leap to G4 COMPREHENSIVE. However, the G4 reporting decision is not about how many indicators B level reporters ticked in the past, but whether they have mature sustainability processes in their organization and have done the work (or are prepared to do the work) to address material focus in their value chain, and are ready to talk about this in the context of sustainability reporting. If yes, COMPREHENSIVE may be within reach.

At the DMA and SSD level, the degree of transparency and stretch in both CORE and COMPRHEHENSIVE versions is largely determined by the selection of material issues: more issues, more disclosure.

What should you do?

Change your mindset. You cannot report at the level of G4 with a G3 mindset. Companies should move away from the approach of deciding which indicators can be reported, and then deciding which Application Level to adopt. COMPREHENSIVE is not a prize – it's intended to be a genuine reflection of the maturity of the company on its sustainability journey. With G4, companies should first think about their role in society and their material impacts. Companies should have some level of embedded stakeholder engagement which informs the selection of material issues, as well as a sustainability program which tracks key impacts and metrics. If companies can demonstrate this level of maturity, they are ready for G4.

A word about format. As online has become a dominant medium of communication these days, you should consider making your G4 fully accessible online and mobile-ready via an app for smartphones and tablets. Getting your report to people that want or need to use it has never been easier. App it!

A word about feedback. G4 provides a greater opportunity to engage with stakeholders. As the report is more focused on material issues, and therefore more meaningful (and possibly comprehensible) to stakeholders, companies should redouble efforts to ensure that feedback is proactively sought, rather than just ticking the box in the GRI Index that requires a contact point. If the report is online, an opportunity exists to provide easy ways for stakeholders to submit comments and suggestions. Also, make sure that the contact point for queries and feedback is an actual contact point. There is nothing more frustrating for a stakeholder, and more trust-eroding, than taking the time to submit feedback to a company on their report and receiving no response.

....

CHAPTER 3

The Language of G4

GRI REPORTING FRAMEWORKS have a language all of their own and, in this book, I have had little choice but to use this language even though, in some cases, the words and phrases are a bit cult-like and have the effect of creating a verbal mystique around sustainability reporting. If you hear anyone ever talking about Material Aspect Boundaries or Specific Standard Disclosures, you will know they have been GRI G4 indoctrinated. However, as this is the language, we need to use it, or we end up in the Tower of Babel. Therefore, I reproduce some of the key terms from the G4 Glossary that you cannot appreciate G4 without understanding, where relevant, with translations in to English.

Aspect

'*The word Aspect is used in the Guidelines to refer to the list of subjects covered by the Guidelines.*' In English, this means that G4 divides up all possible sustainability topics that might be relevant to any company into Categories and Aspects. A Category is composed of several Aspects. There are many more topics than the GRI covers in G4. The ones that G4 has selected to include as generic topics most widely relevant to the majority of companies are called Aspects.

Aspect Boundary

'*Refers to the description of where impacts occur for each material Aspect. In setting the Aspect Boundaries, an organization should consider impacts within and outside of the organization. Aspect Boundaries vary based on the Aspects reported.*' In English, this means that not all material issues are created equal. In some cases, the material issue may be relevant to the internal operations of a company, in others, it may be relevant in the extended supply chain – you might not have a child labor problem in your own factory (internal), but you might have this problem in outsourced factories (external). The Boundary of the Aspect is the place your material issue is relevant. In short, Aspect Boundary.

General Standard Disclosures

'*General Standard Disclosures offer a description of the organization and the reporting process.*' No translation needed. Except that these disclosures are not very general and not very standard. There are 58 General Standard Disclosures in the G4 framework.

Impact

'*In the Guidelines, unless otherwise stated the term "impact" refers to significant economic, environmental and social impacts that are: positive, negative, actual, potential, direct, indirect, short term, long term, intended, unintended.*' Translation: what happens when your business activities affect society and the environment.

Material Aspects

'*Material Aspects are those that reflect the organization's significant economic, environmental and social impacts; or that substantively influence the assessments and decisions of stakeholders.*' Translation: the most important sustainability issues for your business and for your stakeholders.

Reporting Principle

'*Concepts that describe the outcomes a report should achieve and that guide decisions made throughout the reporting process, such as which*

Indicators to respond to, and how to respond to them.' Translation: basic approaches that anchor the content of your report in line with stakeholder expectations.

Scope

'The range of Aspects covered in a report.' Translation: the coverage of issues you select to report on.

Specific Standard Disclosures

'Specific Standard Disclosures offer information on the organization's management and performance related to material Aspects.' Translation: Performance Indicators.

Stakeholders

'Stakeholders are defined as entities or individuals that can reasonably be expected to be significantly affected by the organization's activities, products, and services; and whose actions can reasonably be expected to affect the ability of the organization to successfully implement its strategies and achieve its objectives. This includes entities or individuals whose rights under law or international conventions provide them with legitimate claims vis-à-vis the organization. Stakeholders can include those who are invested in the organization (such as employees, shareholders, suppliers) as well as those who have other relationships to the organization (such as vulnerable groups within local communities, civil society).' Translation: people and groups who influence your business and are influenced by your business.

Topic

'The word topic is used in the Guidelines to refer to any possible sustainability subject.' Translation: anything that is a sustainability issue for any company, and not defined specifically in G4 as an Aspect, is a topic.

....

CHAPTER 4

What's Different About G4 Versus G3?

IN A NUTSHELL, here are the key changes. This section is short and sweet, as G4 is less about technicalities and more about essence. But you ought to know what is different, especially if you are transitioning from current reporting. Below is the condensed version. The full version is in the remaining sections of this book, with commentaries.

- **Reporting levels** have changed to CORE and COMPREHENSIVE for adherence to G4 guidelines to be 'in accordance'. There are more General Standard Disclosures at COMPREHENSIVE level. For both levels, a materiality assessment should be undertaken and a number of topics selected as Material Aspects, and these form the basis of the remaining report content. The selection depends on the company and its stakeholders, and applies to CORE and COMPREHENSIVE level reporting equally. No '+' is now awarded for assurance.

- **Core and Add disclosures** are now no longer differentiated. In G4, all Performance Indicators carry equal weight and the selection of indicators to report is determined by a materiality process and the reporting level, and not pre-defined by the GRI framework. In practice, this means that companies reporting at COMPREHENSIVE level will be required to report more indicators per Material Aspect. For example, if a company selects the Material Aspect 'Product Service and Labelling' in the Product Responsibility category of Specific Standard Disclosures, the company will report on three indicators (G4-PR3, G4-PR4, G4-PR5) whereas in G3 only one (PR3) was core and therefore required to meet Application Level A. In G3.1 overall, 29 of the 84 performance indicators were labelled 'additional' and not therefore required at G3 Application Level A. In G4, all these indicators now carry the same weight, but only if they are part of a selected Material Aspect.

- **General Standard Disclosures (GSDs)** have been expanded and changed as can be seen in Figure 3. The highlights are as follows:

  - Two labor disclosures (G3 LA1 and G3 LA4), now required, previously optional. These cover employee numbers and collective bargaining.

  - Fifteen entirely or extensively modified disclosures in the governance and remuneration category (G4-34–G4-55) requiring much detailed information not previously included.

  - Requirement to describe the organization's supply chain (G4-12).

  - Requirement to list process for determining material topics and listing them (G4-18, G4-19).

  - Disclosure of where the Material Aspect occurs in the organization (G4-21), including whether internal or external to the organization.

- Two new disclosures about ethics (G4-57 and G4-58) focusing on grievance mechanisms.

• **Disclosure on Management Approach (DMA)** has been changed. Instead of a specific DMA for every Aspect, material or otherwise, reporters must now make a DMA for a specific Material Aspect OR a group of Material Aspects, depending on what has been selected for the report content. (If several Aspects in the same category have been selected as material, then the DMA may apply to the entire category, rather than each of the Aspects individually.) G4 divides the DMAs into Generic DMA and Specific DMA. The Generic DMA, which should be applied consistently for all Material Aspects (or group of Aspects) is set out in G4-DMA (G4IM, p. 64) and has three requirements: why an impact is material, how the organization manages the Material Aspect or its impacts and an evaluation of the management approach. This is relevant for any material topic selected, even if it is not one of the G4 pre-prepared Material Aspects. For example, if an alcohol company selects responsible drinking as a Material Topic, which is not an Aspect as included in the GRI list, then a DMA is still required for this Topic. In addition to the Generic DMA reporting requirement, the G4 Implementation Manual includes specific guidance for some of the Material Aspects listed (G4IM, p. 62), but not for all. This is called Aspect-specific guidance. For Material Aspects selected by the reporting company, where guidance is available, G4 reporters are encouraged to use this guidance, although it is not required to be 'In Accordance'. See Figure 4 for a list of the pre-prepared Material Aspects listed in G4 (G4IM, p. 64).

- **Boundaries** in G4 should now be Aspect Specific. This means, for any Material Aspect selected, the reporting company must define whether the impact is internal or external to the organization (disclosures G4-20 and G4-21). This means companies have to consider more than just their internal operations and look for broader impacts of their activities, and include these considerations in their reporting.

- **Specific Standard Disclosures (SSDs)** contain many changes in G4, which will be relevant to each reporter depending on the Material Aspects selected to be included in the report. Each SSD starts with a DMA (see above). Then, for each Material Aspect, there is a list of prescribed Performance Indicators. Of course, you can add more if you wish! Overall, G4 contains 15% more indicators than G3 (see Figure 5), so you have a bigger pot to choose from.

Many Performance Indicators have been changed or modified in G4, and several new ones are added. I address the detailed changes in a later section – Key things to note about Specific Standard Disclosures – and include a full list of G4 Indicators by Category and Aspect with relevant explanations. In Figure 6, I include a reference list of indicators with the corresponding former G3/G3.1 indicators, the existence of specific additional reporting guidance and a note to linkage between UN Global Compact principles and OECD Guidelines for Multinational Enterprises. Just a few highlights for the time being:

- **Economic** indicators have remained largely unchanged, with some minor modifications to G3 indicators.

- **Environmental** indicators have been quite substantially modified. Energy consumption is now one indicator (G4-EN3) covering Scope 1 and Scope 2, while G4-EN4 is a new indicator requiring Scope 3 data. Intensity has been added for energy consumption (G4-EN3) and for greenhouse gas emissions (G4-EN18), a new requirement reflecting alignment with the Greenhouse Gas Protocol (GHG Protocol) of the World Business Council for Sustainable Development (WBCSD) and the World Resources Institute (WRI), and adopted by the Carbon Disclosure Project. Three new indicators have been added (G4-EN32, 33, 34) covering environmental impacts in the supply chain and environmental grievance mechanisms. Former EN14, a superfluous indicator on biodiversity, has been deleted.

- **Labor** indicators have been augmented by three new disclosures (G4-LA14, 15, 16) which relate to labor practices in the supply chain and grievance mechanisms. Two labor indicators from G3 (LA1 and LA4) now appear as standard reporting requirements at CORE and COMPREHENSIVE level as part of the GSDs.

- **Human rights** indicators have remained largely unchanged with just one addition (G4-HR11) which relates to significant actual and potential negative human rights impacts in the supply chain and actions taken.

- **Society** indicators have reduced by two indicators (G3 SO5 and SO10, public policy and prevention and mitigation measures in communities) but increased by three indicators (G4-SO9, 10, 11), similar to the three added in the environment, labor and human rights categories, covering screening of suppliers and grievance mechanisms.

- **Product responsibility** indicators remain largely unchanged, with some minor modifications to existing indicators.

What should you do?

You should not do anything at this stage. Don't work from the indicators backwards. Work from a materiality process forwards. The changes from G3/3.1 to G4 are actually fairly irrelevant (though I knew you would want to know what they are, so I included them). At best, knowing the changes helps you understand the measure of the transition you are making. But it's not your start point. You should start with G4 and how it meets the current stage of your sustainability journey. Therefore, proceed to the next chapter, How Do You Start Writing a G4 Report?

In the meantime you should know that G3 will become officially obsolete at the end of 2015. Until then (two reporting cycles), companies can still use the G3 or G3.1 Framework. It is not yet clear whether GRI will offer a report-check service for this entire period for Application Level Checks for G3 reports, or whether there will be a checking service for new G4 reports.

'Focusing on materiality and recognizing a more focused report format with the G4 will allow more organizations to manage and report on their key business priorities while providing a heightened degree of societal transparency. Broadening the benefits of sustainability reporting will entice more use and provide more in-depth substance.' DR GLENN FROMMER, HEAD OF CORPORATE SUSTAINABILITY, MASS TRANSIT RAILWAY CORPORATION LTD

Comparison tables

FIGURE 3. Comparison of G3 and G4 General Disclosures.

G4	Disclosure*	Required at CORE	Required at COMPREHENSIVE	Corresponding Disclosure in G3	Required at Application Level C	Required at Application Level B or A
STRATEGY AND ANALYSIS						
G4-1	CEO statement	✓	✓	1.1	✓	✓
G4-2	Risks and impacts	✗	✓	1.2	✗	✓
ORGANIZATIONAL PROFILE						
G4-3	Name of reporting organization	✓	✓	2.1	✓	✓
G4-4	Products	✓	✓	2.2	✓	✓
G4-5	HQ location	✓	✓	2.4	✓	✓
G4-6	Countries of operation	✓	✓	2.5	✓	✓
G4-7	Legal form	✓	✓	2.6	✓	✓
G4-8	Markets served	✓	✓	2.7	✓	✓
G4-9	Scale of organization	✓	✓	2.8	✓	✓
G4-10	Employee statistics	✓	✓	LA1	Optional	✓
G4-11	Collective bargaining	✓	✓	LA4	Optional	✓
G4-12	Supply chain	✓	✓	NEW	N/A	N/A
G4-13	Changes in reporting period	✓	✓	2.9	✓	✓
G4-14	Precautionary approach	✓	✓	4.11	✗	✓
G4-15	External charters	✓	✓	4.12	✗	✓
G4-16	Membership of associations	✓	✓	4.13	✗	✓
IDENTIFIED MATERIAL ASPECTS AND BOUNDARIES						
G4-17	List all entities	✓	✓	2.3	✓	✓
G4-18	Process for defining aspects	✓	✓	3.5	✓	✓
G4-19	List Material Aspects	✓	✓	NEW	N/A	N/A
G4-20	Aspect Boundaries – internal	✓	✓	3.6,3.7,3.8	✓	✓
G4-21	Aspect Boundaries - external	✓	✓	3.6,3.7,3.8	✓	✓
G4-22	Restatements	✓	✓	3.10	✓	✓
G4-23	Significant changes	✓	✓	3.11	✓	✓
STAKEHOLDER ENGAGEMENT						
G4-24	List of stakeholder groups	✓	✓	4.14	✓	✓
G4-25	Basis for selection of stakeholders	✓	✓	4.15	✓	✓
G4-26	Approach to stakeholder engagement	✓	✓	4.16	✗	✓
G4-27	Key topics raised by stakeholders	✓	✓	4.17	✗	✓
REPORT PROFILE						
G4-28	Reporting period	✓	✓	3.1	✓	✓
G4-29	Date of most recent report	✓	✓	3.2	✓	✓
G4-30	Reporting cycle	✓	✓	3.3	✓	✓
G4-31	Contact point	✓	✓	3.4	✓	✓
G4-32	Content Index	✓	✓	3.12	✓	✓
G4-33	Practice regarding assurance	✓	✓	3.13	✗	✓

WHAT'S DIFFERENT ABOUT
G4 VERSUS G3?

G4	Disclosure*	Required at CORE	Required at COMPREHENSIVE	Corresponding Disclosure in G3	Required at Application Level C	Required at Application Level B or A
GOVERNANCE						
G4-34	Governance structure	☑	☑	4.1	☑	☑
G4-35	Process for delegation to executives	☒	☑	NEW	N/A	N/A
G4-36	Executive responsible for sustainability	☒	☑	NEW	N/A	N/A
G4-37	Stakeholder-Board consultation	☒	☑	4.4	☑	☑
G4-38	Composition of Board	☒	☑	4.3	☑	☑
G4-39	Chair of Board –executive role	☒	☑	4.2	☑	☑
G4-40	Director nomination process	☒	☑	4.7	☒	☑
G4-41	Managing conflict of interest	☒	☑	4.6	☒	☑
G4-42	Updating mission and values	☒	☑	NEW	N/A	N/A
G4-43	Board sustainability knowledge	☒	☑	NEW	N/A	N/A
G4-44	Evaluating Board performance	☒	☑	4.10	☒	☑
G4-45	Board role – sustainability risks	☒	☑	4.9	☒	☑
G4-46	Risk management effectiveness	☒	☑	NEW	N/A	N/A
G4-47	Sustainability review frequency	☒	☑	4.9	☒	☑
G4-48	Approving sustainability report	☒	☑	NEW	N/A	N/A
G4-49	Communicating concerns to Board	☒	☑	NEW	N/A	N/A
G4-50	Concerns dealt with by Board	☒	☑	NEW	N/A	N/A
G4-51	Remuneration policy: Board and Execs	☒	☑	NEW	N/A	N/A
G4-52	Remuneration process	☒	☑	NEW	N/A	N/A
G4-53	Stakeholder input- remuneration	☒	☑	NEW	N/A	N/A
G4-54	Compensation ratio execs-average	☒	☑	NEW	N/A	N/A
G4-55	Compensation increase	☒	☑	NEW	N/A	N/A
ETHICS AND INTEGRITY						
G4-56	Code of Ethics	☑	☑	4.8	☒	☑
G4-57	Helplines	☒	☑	NEW	N/A	N/A
G4-58	Reporting ethical concerns	☒	☑	NEW	N/A	N/A

Note: Author's shorthand used in above disclosure references, e.g. "Board" is used where G4 uses "highest governing body" and "sustainability" is used where G4 refers to "economic, environmental and social impacts". For full and correct disclosure requirements, see the G4 Implementation Manual.

....

FIGURE 4. Material Aspects covered by G4.

Comparison of G4 Aspects to G3.1			
Aspects Defined and Detailed in G4	Covered in G3.1	Aspects Defined and Detailed in G4	Covered in G3.1
Category: Economic (4)		**Category: Social. Sub-Category: Human Rights (10)**	
Economic Performance	☑	Investment	☑
Market Presence	☑	Non-discrimination	☑
Indirect Economic Impacts	☑	Freedom of Association and Collective Bargaining	☑
Procurement Practices	☒	Child Labor	☑
Category: Environmental (12)		Forced or Compulsory Labor	☑
Materials	☑	Security Practices	☑
Energy	☑	Indigenous Rights	☑
Water	☑	Assessment	☑
Biodiversity	☑	Supplier Human Rights Assessment	☒
Emissions	☑	Human Rights Grievance Mechanisms	☒
Effluents and Waste	☑	**Category: Social. Sub-Category: Society (7)**	
Products and Services	☑	Local Communities	☑
Compliance	☑	Anti-corruption	☑
Transport	☑	Public Policy	☑
Overall	☑	Anti-competitive Behavior	☑
Supplier Environmental Assessment	☒	Compliance	☑
Environmental Grievance Mechanisms	☒	Supplier Assessment for Impacts on Society	☒
Category: Social. Sub-Category: Labor Practices and Decent Work (8)		Grievance Mechanisms for Impacts on Society	☒
Employment	☑	**Category: Social. Sub-Category: Product Responsibility (5)**	
Labor/Management Relations	☑	Customer Health and Safety	☑
Occupational Health and Safety	☑	Product and Service Labeling	☑
Training and Education	☑	Marketing Communications	☑
Diversity and Equal Opportunity	☑	Customer Privacy	☑
Equal Remuneration for Women and Men	☑	Compliance	☑
Supplier Assessment for Labor Practices	☒		
Labor Practices Grievance Mechanisms	☒		
G4: 46 Aspects. G3: 37 Aspects			

'Sustainability reporting which supports and drives strategic understanding and integration can only be a good thing for both sustainability and companies. G4 moves reporting from outside the company to part of business practice. It stands to make a meaningful contribution to the development of sustainable companies, not just sustainability reporting companies.' JOSS TANTRAM, FOUNDING PARTNER, TERRAFINITI LLP, A PIONEERING SUSTAINABILITY AND SYSTEMS CONSULTANCY

'The myriad of rankings, ratings, certifications and reporting frameworks not only confound sustainability professionals, they compete for stakeholder attention. The result is confusion and reduced credibility. An increasing number of companies – recognizing the increasing number of hours it takes to respond to information requests – are looking at streamlining their efforts and reporting by focusing (and increasingly more exclusively) on rankings that are the most credible among their stakeholders and that offer them a comprehensive evaluation of their efforts across environment, social, governance and ethical considerations and. That is driving tremendous interest in G4.' JOHN T. FRIEDMAN, CORPORATE CITIZENSHIP COMMUNICATIONS DIRECTOR, SODEXO GROUP

FIGURE 5. Changes in the number of Performance Indicators.

Numbers of performance indicators by category			
	G4	G3.1	G3
Economic	9	9	9
Environmental	34	30	30
Social: Labor Practices	16	15	14
Social: Human Rights	12	11	9
Social Society	11	10	8
Social: Product Responsibility	9	9	9
TOTAL	91	84	79

'I think G4 is a great step forward; reports will be more useful for both companies and stakeholders because only material aspects will be reported. Reports will feature only important things that matter. The combination of materiality and supply chain (through the aspect boundaries) is one of the highlights, plus the new indicators of governance, ethics and integrity (especially interesting in Spain where companies lack credibility and trust). I am interested in the G4.54 indicator that shows the ratio of the highest remuneration to the median remuneration of a company. I miss some indicator that shows the company's contribution to common good (tough one!), and the incorporation of critical views in the reports.' JUAN VILLAMAYOR, CSR CONSULTANT FROM BARCELONA, http://juanvillamayor.com

'The new G4 will be a tough burden for a small or medium sized enterprise (SME). How many SMEs have a person with the understanding – and the time – to read 300 pages of G4 texts? So an SME should take a consultant . . . but as few SME will engage in this journey, consultants who can usefully implement G4 for SMEs will only emerge slowly. I already hear the call for subsidies for supporting SMEs going for G4 . . . but wouldn't it be better to design a SME-oriented standard from the outset? I think SMEs have the largest innovation potential of an economy, and both SMEs and the society at large can profit enormously from sustainably-oriented SMEs. We all would profit from a slim-line 'SME-G4'. ARTHUR BRAUNSCHWEIG, E2 MANAGEMENT CONSULTING AG

'G4 provides the basis to professionalize reporting processes to focus on the material issues for a company's own sustainability. As an assurance provider, we strongly emphasize the need for professionalizing the issue identification processes to achieve continuous credible reporting. It is time for implementation now.' WIM BARTELS, PARTNER AT KPMG THE NETHERLANDS, GLOBAL HEAD OF SUSTAINABILITY ASSURANCE AT KPMG

FIGURE 6. Specific Standard Disclosures by Category and Aspect.

CATEGORY: ECONOMIC

G4	ASPECT	Disclosure	Corresponding Disclosure in G3/G3.1	Specific Aspect Guidance Available	UNGC Principle Link	OECD Chapter Link
G4-EC1	Economic Performance	Economic value	EC1			
G4-EC2		Climate change risks	EC2			V, XI
G4-EC3		Benefit plan coverage	EC3			
G4-EC4		Finance from government	EC4			
G4-EC5	Market Presence	Entry wage ratio	EC5			
G4-EC6		Local management	EC7			
G4-EC7	Indirect Economic Impacts	Infrastructure investments	EC8	G4IM Page 78		
G4-EC8		Indirect economic impacts	EC9			
G4-EC9	Procurement Practices	Local suppliers	EC6	G4IM Page 82		

CATEGORY: ENVIRONMENT

G4	ASPECT	Disclosure	Corresponding Disclosure in G3/G3.1	Specific Aspect Guidance Available	UNGC Principle Link	OECD Chapter Link
G4-EN1	Materials	Materials by weight or volume	EN1		Principles 7,8,9	VI
G4-EN2		Recycled input materials	EN2			
G4-EN3	Energy	Energy consumption (Scope 1+2)	EN3+ EN4			
G4-EN4		Energy consumption (Scope 3)	NEW			
G4-EN5		Energy intensity	NEW	G4IM page 88	Principles 7,8,9	VI
G4-EN6		Energy consumption reduction	EN5+EN7			
G4-EN7		Products and services energy reduction	EN6			
G4-EN8	Water	Water withdrawal by source	EN8		Principles 7,8,9	VI
G4-EN9		Water sources affected by water withdrawal	EN9			
G4-EN10		Water recycled and reused	EN10			
G4-EN11	Biodiversity	Sites in or near areas of high biodiversity	EN11		Principles 7,8,9	VI
G4-EN12		Impacts on biodiversity	EN12	G4IM Page 10		
G4-EN13		Habitats protected or restored	EN13			
G4-EN14		IUCN Red List species	EN15			
G4-EN15	Emissions	GHG emissions (Scope 1)	EN16		Principles 7,8,9	VI
G4-EN16		GHG emissions (Scope 2)	EN16			
G4-EN17		GHG emissions (Scope 3)	EN17			
G4-EN18		GHG emissions intensity	NEW	G4IM page 106		
G4-EN19		Reduction of GHG emissions	EN18			
G4-EN20		Ozone-depleting substances (ODS)	EN19			
G4-EN21		NOX, SOX, and other emissions	EN20			
G4-EN22	Effluents and Waste	Water discharge	EN21		Principles 7,8,9	VI
G4-EN23		Waste by type and disposal	EN22			
G4-EN24		Significant spills	EN23			
G4-EN25		Hazardous waste	EN24			
G4-EN26		Biodiversity affected by runoff	EN25			
G4-EN27	Products and Services	Mitigation of environmental impacts of products and services	EN26		Principles 7,8,9	VI
G4-EN28		Products and packaging materials reclaimed	EN27			
G4-EN29	Compliance	Environmental fines and sanctions	EN28		Principles 7,8,9	VI
G4-EN30	Transport	Environmental impacts of transporting products	EN29		Principles 7,8,9	VI
G4-EN31	Overall	Environmental investments	EN30		Principles 7,8,9	VI
G4-EN32	Supplier Environmental	New suppliers screened for environment	NEW	G4IM pages 136-137	Principles 7,8,9	VI
G4-EN33		Supply chain environmental impacts	NEW			
G4-EN34	Environmental Grievance Mechanisms	Environmental grievances	NEW	G4IM page 140	Principles 7,8,9	VI

WHAT'S DIFFERENT ABOUT G4 VERSUS G3?

\multicolumn{6}{l}{CATEGORY: SOCIAL. SUB CATEGORY : LABOR PRACTICES AND DECENT WORK}						
G4	ASPECT	Disclosure	Corresponding Disclosure in G3/G3.1	Specific Aspect Guidance Available	UNGC Principle Link	OECD Chapter Link
G4-LA1	Employment	New employee hires and employee turnover by age group, gender, and region	LA2	G4IM pages 144-145	Principle 6	V
G4-LA2		Benefits provided to full-time employees	LA3			
G4-LA3		Return to work and retention after parental leave	LA15			
G4-LA4	Labor / Management Relations	Notice periods regarding operational changes	LA5		Principles 3, 6	V
G4-LA5	Occupational Health and Safety	Workforce represented in health and safety committees	LA6	G4IM page 151	Principle 6	V, VI
G4-LA6		Injury and rates of injury, occupational diseases, lost days, and absenteeism	LA7			
G4-LA7		Workers with high incidence risk of diseases	NEW			
G4-LA8		Health and safety topics covered in agreements with trade unions	LA9			
G4-LA9	Training and Education	Hours of training per year per employee	LA10		Principle 6	V, VI
G4-LA10		Programs for skills management and lifelong learning	LA11			
G4-LA11		Employees receiving regular performance and career development reviews	LA12			
G4-LA12	Diversity and Equal Opportunity	Composition of governance bodies	LA13		Principle 6	V
G4-LA13	Equal Remuneration for Women and Men	Ratio of basic salary and remuneration of women to men	LA14	G4IM page 165	Principle 6	V
G4-LA14	Supplier Assessment for Labor Practices	Percentage of new suppliers that were screened using labor practices criteria	NEW	G4IM pages 167-168	Principle 6	V
G4-LA15		Negative impacts for labor practices in the supply chain and actions taken	NEW			
G4-LA16	Labor Practices Grievance Mechanisms	Number of grievances about labor practices	NEW	G4IM page 171	Principle 6	V, VII

CATEGORY: SOCIAL. SUB CATEGORY : HUMAN RIGHTS

G4	ASPECT	Disclosure	Corresponding Disclosure in G3/G3.1	Specific Aspect Guidance Available	UNGC Principle Link	OECD Chapter Link
G4-HR1	Investment	Human rights clauses or screening in investment agreements and contracts	HR1	G4IM page 175	Principles 1,2	IV
G4-HR2		Employee training on human rights	HR3			
G4-HR3	Non-discrimination	Incidents of discrimination and corrective actions taken	HR4		Principles 1,2,3, 6	IV,V
G4-HR4	Freedom of Association	Significant risk of freedom of association in operations and suppliers	HR5	G4IM page 180	Principles 1,2,4	IV,V
G4-HR5	Child Labor	Significant risk ofincidents of child labor in operations and suppliers	HR6		Principles 1,2,5	IV,V
G4-HR6	Forced or Compulsory Labor	Significant risk of incidents of forced labor at operations and suppliers	HR7		Principles 1,2	IV,V
G4-HR7	Security Practices	measures to contribute to the elimination of all forms of forced or compulsory labor	HR8		Principles 1,2	IV
G4-HR8	Indigenous Rights	Violations involving rights of indigenous peoples	HR9		Principles 1,2	IV
G4-HR9	Assessment	Operations that have been subject to human rights assessments	HR10		Principles 1,2	IV
G4-HR10	Supplier Human Rights Assessment	New suppliers screened for human rights	HR2	G4IM pages 192-193	Principles 1,2	IV
G4-HR11		Negative human rights impacts in supply chain	NEW			
G4-HR12	Human Rights Grievance Mechanisms	Grievances about human rights impacts	HR11	G4IM page 196	Principles 1,2	IV

CATEGORY: SOCIAL. SUB CATEGORY : SOCIETY

G4	ASPECT	Disclosure	Corresponding Disclosure in G3/G3.1	Specific Aspect Guidance Available	UNGC Principle Link	OECD Chapter Link
G4-SO1	Local Communities	Local community engagement, impact assessments, and development programs	SO1	G4IM page 199	Principle 1	IV,V, VI
G4-SO2		Negative impacts on local communities	SO9, SO10			
G4-SO3	Anti-corruption	Risks related to corruption	SO2	G4IM page 205	Principle 10	VII
G4-SO4		Communication and training on anti-corruption	SO3			
G4-SO5		Confirmed incidents of corruption	SO4			
G4-SO6	Public Policy	Political contributions	SO5, SO6	G4IM page 205	Principle 10	VII
G4-SO7	Anti-competitive Behavior	Anti-competitive behavior	SO7			X, XI
G4-SO8	Compliance	Fines for non-compliance with laws	SO8			X, XI
G4-SO9	Supplier Assessment for Impacts on Society	New suppliers screened for impacts on society	NEW	G4IM pages 215-216		IV, VI, VII,X
G4-SO10		Negative impacts on society in the supply chain	NEW			
G4-SO11	Grievance Mechanisms for Impacts on Society	Grievances about impacts on society	NEW	G4IM page 219		IV, VI, VII, X

WHAT'S DIFFERENT ABOUT
G4 VERSUS G3?

CATEGORY: SOCIAL. SUB CATEGORY : PRODUCT RESPONSIBILITY						
G4	ASPECT	Disclosure	Corresponding Disclosure in G3/G3.1	Specific Aspect Guidance Available	UNGC Principle Link	OECD Chapter Link
G4-PR1	Customer Health and Safety	Health and safety impacts product assessments	PR1	G4IM page 222		VI, VIII
G4-PR2		Non-compliance concerning the health and safety impacts of products	PR2			
G4-PR3	Product and Service Labeling	Product and service information and labeling	PR3	G4IM page 225		VIII
G4-PR4		Non-compliance with regulations concerning product labeling	PR4			
G4-PR5		Surveys measuring customer satisfaction	PR5			
G4-PR6	Marketing Communications	Sale of banned or disputed products	PR6			VIII
G4-PR7		Non-compliance with regulations concerning marketing communications	PR7			VIII
G4-PR8	Customer Privacy	Complaints regarding breaches of customer privacy and losses of customer data	PR8			VIII
G4-PR9	Compliance	Fines for non-compliance concerning the provision and use of products and services	PR9			VIII

Notes:

The cross-references to UNGC Principles and OECD Guidelines for Multinational Enterprises are listed in the GRI Manual G4 Reporting Principles and Standard Disclosures – I have reproduced them here for reference but I did not check that they are correct!

The disclosures in this table have been shortened for the purposes of fitting the key subject onto these small pages. For the full disclosure wording, refer to the G4 Implementation Manual.

....

CHAPTER 5

How Do You Start Writing a G4 Report?

I BELIEVE THERE ARE SEVEN prerequisites for G4 reporting, as follows:

1. *Leadership* with intelligence, values and a determination to run a successful, sustainable business. Leadership should be apparent in the company practice to date, with elements of good governance, insistence on an ethical culture and positive business practices.

2. *A team*, which supports the leadership, that is capable of translating this into sustainability strategy, policies, programs and actions, with supporting infrastructures, partnerships and communications. Often this team might be headed by a Chief Sustainability Officer or CSR Manager, but not necessarily.

3. *A process for engaging stakeholders* about the way the business impacts them, their community and our planet. This should be at least, in part, a structured process, which is open, documented, and ensures genuine, relevant dialog that leads to conclusions which can be used to determine key areas of stakeholder interest, expectation and concern, and ultimately, influence business decisions.

4. *A process for identifying and prioritizing material issues.* This should be informed by business strategy, stakeholder input and a broad

review of relevant sustainability topics. Following identification of the topics, there should be a process for prioritization according to the G4 dual criteria of 1) significance of the business's value chain economic, environmental, and social impacts and 2) influence of the business value chain impacts on stakeholder assessments and decisions. This prioritization is best done with external stakeholder input, as well as internal management input. The result of this process is the fifth element that should be in place – a Materiality Matrix – which is one of the pivotal factors in determining the content for a G4 report.

5. *A Materiality Matrix* which shows the position of prioritized sustainability topics in alignment with the Material Aspects defined in G4. Where there is alignment, the minimum reporting requirement will be clear (both DMA and SSD). Where there are material topics which are not aligned with the G4 Material Aspects, the reporting company should still report DMA and select relevant indicators for measuring performance and reporting. At this point, the boundary of selected Material Aspects should be determined – internal, external or a mixture of both.

6. *A decision how to report.* This will involve an assessment of the readiness of the reporting company to disclose on GSDs as well as Material Aspects and Topics, based on the level of transparency the company is prepared to demonstrate and the maturity of the sustainability processes and performance. For example, it may be that significant supporting information is available relating to the priority Material Aspects, but that the company is uncomfortable for whatever reason about disclosing

at this time. It may be that new Material Aspects have been identified for which complete information is not available. The company may be an experienced reporter at GRI A level, or may never have reported before. The G4 Decision Matrix (Figure 7) is not an exhaustive decision-making tool but may help in defining the company's approach to reporting.

7. *A plan.* And a copy of the G4 Reporting Principles and Implementation Manuals (if you are in any of the three higher quadrants of Figure 7). And this book, of course! And the relevant budget and resources necessary to go through all the stages of developing the concept, content and format for publication of your report.

FIGURE 7. The G4 Decision Matrix.

The G4 DECISION MATRIX

MATURITY

REPORT G4 CORE
- You are probably an SME or a private company.
- You probably have reported before using GRI at C or possibly B level.
- You have or can develop a Materiality Process identifying where material impacts occur (Boundaries)
- Enough information and data is available or can be generated to report at CORE LEVEL.
- CORE level transparency meets known stakeholder requirements.
- You see reporting as an investment in your sustainable business.

REPORT G4 COMPREHENSIVE
- You are probably a large, complex company, publicly traded, and have a record of sustainability reporting using GRI at B or A level.
- You have or can develop a Materiality Process identifying where material impacts occur (Boundaries).
- Investors use your ESG data for analysis purposes.
- Stakeholders demand extensive disclosure
- Enough information and data is available or can be generated to report at COMPREHENSIVE level.
- You see reporting as an investment in your sustainable business.

REPORT NOT GRI
- Your company is probably at the start of your sustainability journey and you have probably not published a Sustainability Report yet.
- You aim for more transparency but information gathering infrastructure, stakeholder engagement and materiality assessments are not in place, though you can record some progress.
- You do not believe G4 is the best framework, or prefer to report using other formats.

REPORT G4 NO LEVEL
- You could be any company. You have made some progress along your sustainability journey. You may have already published a Sustainability Report.
- Your company understands the value of transparency but insufficient information is available and cannot yet be generated to report at CORE level, or simply, leadership is not aligned on what and how to report.
- You have not yet developed a Materiality Process and this will take some time.

TRANSPARENCY

I am tempted to add an eighth element, which is a toolkit of competencies and attributes which include: endless patience, collaboration, cooperation, eye for detail, great storytelling, humility, appreciation, wisdom, passion, honesty, integrity, authenticity, persuasion and many others. But that was true of reporting before G4 was born, so we'll leave this list as 'important to note' and not a specific G4 reporting process element.

Now that you have your plan, having ensured that the seven G4 reporting elements are in place, you start getting into the detailed work. In the following chapters, we address some of the important points to look at as you work through your reporting process.

....

CHAPTER 6

What To Look For When Developing a G4 Report?

Key things to note about the Reporting Principles

The first G4 booklet, Reporting Principles and Standard Disclosures, now comes in to play. There are two types of principles which should form a basis for your reporting: Principles for Defining Report Content (Figure 8) and Principles for Defining Report Quality (Figure 9). The principles themselves are the same as those in G3, but given the different nature of G4, the application of them may be a little different.

Materiality has been strongly upgraded in G4, and as we have seen, governs the selection of content for the Specific Standard Disclosures. The process, using these principles, recommended by GRI for determining Material Aspects is the Identification-Prioritization-Validation-Review model which is described in GSD G4-18, which also requires disclosure of how the organization has implemented the Reporting Principles for Defining Report Content. The tests, to assess whether the principles are appropriately applied, are listed in the Implementation Manual (pp. 9–13).

Of course, one of the challenges of G4 is that the principles are open to interpretation and adaptation by companies. In terms of *stakeholder inclusiveness*, how a company identifies and prioritizes its stakeholders is not prescribed – most companies have primary stakeholders who are employees, customers and suppliers – but these groups will not always give a full and balanced picture of a company's most serious impacts. Other companies may have specific stakeholder groups which are highly influential and with whom engagement is critical. The selection of stakeholders and how to engage has a direct impact on the selection of material issues.

FIGURE 8. Principles for Defining Report Content.

Principles for Defining Report Content

The report reflects significant economic, environmental and social impacts and substantively influences the assessments and decisions of stakeholders

The report should include coverage of Material Aspects and their Boundaries, sufficient to reflect significant sustainability impacts, and to enable stakeholders to assess the organization's performance.

MATERIALITY   **COMPLETENESS**

STAKEHOLDER INCLUSIVENESS   **SUSTAINABILITY CONTEXT**

The report should identify who are identified as stakeholders or stakeholder groups and provide a response to their reasonable interests and expectations.

The report should present the organization's performance in the wider context of sustainability. This involves discussing the performance of the organization in the context of the limits and demands placed on environmental or social resources at the sector, local, regional, or global level.

Equally, sustainability context can be interpreted liberally, with reference to overriding global trends, or it can be interpreted more specifically, with reference to calculated limitations of natural resources and the company's relative consumption of these. The definition of *completeness* includes reference to impacts which occur inside of and outside of the organization (i.e. in the value chain), identifying where they occur, and covers the scope of issues included in the report and the timeliness of reporting. Here again, interpretation and application will influence the report content. Does the report cover all operations, sites, processes, or are significant geographies or JVs or other activities not included?

FIGURE 9. Principles for defining report quality.

Principles for Defining Report Quality

The report should present an unbiased picture of the organization's performance

The report content should be able to be understood by stakeholders who have a reasonable knowledge of the organization's activities

BALANCE   **CLARITY**
TIMELINESS   **COMPARABILITY**
ACCURACY   **RELIABILITY**

The report should be published on a consistent time schedule, so that stakeholders can look forward to it ☺ Also, it should be published as early as possible after the end of the stated reporting period.

Information in the report should be comparable to past performance and if possible, to other organizations.

Make your report accurate and detailed enough so that your stakeholders can use it to assess your performance.

The information and data in the report should be presented in such a way as can be checked. Your stakeholders want to be able to confirm that you did it right.

Comparability, always an evasive objective of sustainability reporting, has generally been understood primarily as the ability to compare one company's performance with another and deliver what we all like to see, a rank of good, better, best. However, this was never achieved, as even though companies reported on the same indicators, the data was never quite comparable. Why not? Because often the same data was not the same data. Companies became expert at adapting GRI Performance Indicators to their capability or willingness to report, so that a carbon footprint might be presented for a whole organization, or a part of the organization, or might include operations below or over a certain size, or may omit new sites or may use different carbon emission conversion factors. Similarly, even if the data methodology is the same, the sustainability context of the reporting companies is different, so the relevance of a ton of carbon emissions for one company may be quite different from the relevance of that same ton in another company in a different sector, or another company at a different stage on its sustainability journey. While sector comparisons tended to be the closest we could get to some level of comparability, it was always hit and miss. Now in G4 comparability becomes even more elusive.

We may be able to compare material issue selection at some level. If every communications technology company selects 'data privacy' as a material issue, we might conclude that a company which does not is guilty of omission, although different contextual and circumstantial issues, and different stakeholder feedback, may be plausible explanations for different prioritization. As Material Aspect selection influences which indicators are reported, we may find vast differences between companies, even within a sector. This renders comparability across companies virtually impossible at the SSD level. (In practice, we may find that the larger, more complex companies will report on a broader range of issues in any event, so there may be some common ground, but this may be more by chance than by design.) Comparability has thus been relegated to being more about comparing a single company's performance against its own past performance, and drives home the need for consistency over reporting years by individual companies.

The principle of *balance* has also been one to which historically lip service has been paid by many reporters. Despite 'bad news' being one of the most attractive parts for report users, according to a recent survey by **CorporateRegister.com**, both adding credibility and a little spice to the generally overly positive content of sustainability reports, this has often been too hard to handle for most companies. In G4, the balance principle hasn't changed, but will G4 change the application of it? It could do. Given that more explicit description of impacts, more thorough DMAs and high-materiality Performance Indicators are required, it may be harder to hide behind the halo. This will depend on how seriously companies take G4.

As for the other principles, there's nothing new, and no point in adding any further commentary. They are self-explanatory and can be found in the Implementation Manual (pp. 13–16).

What should you do?

Ideally, before you start reporting, you should consider all these principles and what they mean for your company. You should agree how to identify that your report demonstrates these principles in practice, and whether report users will be able to identify them. In the report, you should include a description of your definition and approach to each one. Briefly, of course.

Key things to note about
General Standard Disclosures

General Standard Disclosures form the basis of reporting at both CORE and COMPREHENSIVE level. At CORE level, there are 34 GSDs, four more disclosures than required at G3 Application Level C, and at

COMPREHENSIVE there are 58 GSDs, 16 more disclosures than required at Application Level A. Therefore, the baseline in sustainability reporting has been raised a little, with companies requiring to report more than they had done previously.

The disclosures are organized into seven sections as shown in the table below:

General Standard Disclosures by section	Number of disclosures at CORE level	Number of disclosures at COMPREHENSIVE level
Strategy and Analysis	1	2
Organizational Profile	14	14
Identified Material Aspects and Boundaries	7	7
Stakeholder Engagement	4	4
Report Profile	6	6
Governance	1	22
Ethics and Integrity	1	3
Total	34	58

Some of the changes to the General Standard Disclosures affect all reporters, while some are required only at COMPREHENSIVE level.

New GSDs affecting all reporters

EMPLOYEES: G4-10 and G4-11, in the Organizational Profile section, are now general disclosures where they were previously optional for Application Level B or C reporters.

G4-10 includes detail about the company's workforce in some detail:

- *Report the total number of employees by employment contract and gender.*

- *Report the total number of permanent employees by employment type and gender.*

- *Report the total workforce by employees and supervised workers and by gender.*

- *Report the total workforce by region and gender.*

- *Report whether a substantial portion of the organization's work is performed by workers who are legally recognized as self-employed, or by individuals other than employees or supervised workers, including employees and supervised employees of contractors.*

- *Report any significant variations in employment numbers (such as seasonal variations in employment in the tourism or agricultural industries).*

G4-11 simply requires the number of employees *covered by Collective Bargaining Agreements.* It is often surprising to me how many reports do not include details of the workforce, so this basic requirement is a welcome addition and possibly a new challenge for some reporting companies.

SUPPLY CHAIN: G4-12, a new disclosure in G4, is deceptively simple: *Describe the organization's supply chain.* While G4 includes new definitions of Supply Chain and Suppliers in the G4 Glossary, this disclosure is a little like the question how long is a piece of string? There is no minimum requirement to define where the supply chain starts and where it ends, nor how much detail to include. Meeting this disclosure requirement can be a five minute back-of-the-envelope exercise or the result of detailed discussions and analysis. This is part of the new G4 philosophy – by being less prescriptive in its overall approach, it urges companies to make the best disclosure they can, given their particular circumstances. For smaller companies, the supply chain might be quite a simple affair, while for global operations, it may be horrendously complex. By allowing flexibility within this disclosure requirement, G4 invites companies to deliver the best representation they can at any point in time. It also provides an opportunity for companies to apply the materiality concept to the supply chain. Rather than collect and report data on all suppliers indiscriminately, G4 encourages reporting on the most significant impacts in the supply chain, and the most significant suppliers. It is conceivable that a complex company's first G4 report may contain a brief description of the supply chain which becomes more detailed in future reports. This is essentially a positive approach, though, of course, it leaves the door wide open for companies that are holding onto a G3 mindset (box-ticking) to disclose the minimum in order to be 'In Accordance'.

MATERIALITY: The most significant changes to the General Standard Disclosures are the ones relating to materiality process and definition of material aspects and boundaries. These are pivotal disclosures which display the maturity of a company in its sustainability program and transparency and anchor the content of the report around the most important issues for the company and its stakeholders. These are the key disclosures:

G4-17: List all entities included in the organization's consolidated financial statements or equivalent documents. Report whether any entity included in the organization's consolidated financial statements or equivalent documents is not covered by the report.

G4-18: Explain the process for defining the report content and the Aspect Boundaries. Explain how the organization has implemented the Reporting Principles for Defining Report Content.

G4-19: List all the material Aspects identified in the process for defining report content.

G4-20: For each material Aspect, report the Aspect Boundary within the organization, as follows:

- Report whether the Aspect is material within the organization. If the Aspect is not material for all entities within the organization (as described in G4-17), select one of the following two approaches and report either:

  - The list of entities or groups of entities included in G4-17 for which the Aspect is not material or

  - The list of entities or groups of entities included in G4-17 for which the Aspects is material

- Report any specific limitation regarding the Aspect Boundary within the organization

G4-21: For each material Aspect, report the Aspect Boundary outside the organization, as follows:

- Report whether the Aspect is material outside of the organization

- If the Aspect is material outside of the organization, identify the entities, groups of entities or elements for which the Aspect is material. In addition, describe the geographical location where the Aspect is material for the entities identified

- Report any specific limitation regarding the Aspect Boundary outside the organization

These five disclosures are very powerful. They first of all create the context for the report and align the reporting coverage to a company's financial reports. It's now no longer all that easy to 'ignore' a few operations in different countries, or a few local subsidiaries in your sustainability reporting. A company must ensure its sustainability report references its entire operations, whether or not they are included in the report content. Secondly, the company must describe how it defined and prioritized material issues, while identifying where they are of most impact, inside or outside the organization. G4 contains detailed guidance on internal and external Aspect Boundaries (pp. 34–35 of the Implementation Manual). Anti-corruption, for example, may not be considered a Material Aspect in the main locations of a company where anti-corruption practices and controls are in place, but in the business the company does through its subsidiaries in remote markets which are high corruption risk, anti-corruption may be very relevant. Similarly, child labor may not be an issue in a company, but it may be a problem in the supply chain.

Defining the Aspect Boundary further refines the concept of materiality, making material issues focused, targeted locally relevant and more specifically defined. This is a step in the right direction and guides companies toward more focused reporting. On the other hand, the granular nature of Material Aspect Boundaries as the foundation for the sustainability report may divert attention from underlying trends and broader considerations which might be relevant across the entire organization. Similarly, this hi-res materiality is more susceptible to change every year as business dynamics shift. This means that it could become impossible to achieve continuity in reporting from year to year, which could be confusing for stakeholders.

Finally on materiality, while this is generally positive, the risk is that companies will select Material Aspect Boundaries based on what is easiest to report and not what is expedient to report. It's easy enough to create a reasonably convincing narrative which meets G4 requirements, without having done the detailed work. Stakeholders, especially local stakeholders, will need to be vigilant when using G4 reports, ensuring that they match what is disclosed with what makes sense, given local market knowledge and context.

New GSDs affecting only COMPREHENSIVE reporters

GOVERNANCE AND REMUNERATION: This section has been expanded to include disclosures at an extremely high level of detail which are designed to provide an overview of:

- The governance structure and its composition

- The role of the highest governance body in setting the organization's purpose, values and strategy

- The competencies and performance evaluation of the highest governance body

- The role of the highest governance body in risk management

- The role of the highest governance body in sustainability reporting

- The role of the highest governance body in evaluating economic, environmental and social performance

- Remuneration and incentives

Some of these disclosures, to my mind, are overly detailed, and include ten entirely new disclosures beyond those required in G3 Application Level A. Several others have been modified or expanded. It's worth listing all the governance and remuneration disclosures here:

....

G4-34   Report the governance structure of the organization, including committees of the highest governance body. Identify any committees responsible for decision-making on economic, environmental and social impacts.

....

G4-35   Report the process for delegating authority for economic, environmental and social topics from the highest governance body to senior executives and other employees.

....

G4-36   Report whether the organization has appointed an executive-level position or positions with responsibility for economic, environmental and social topics, and whether post-holders report directly to the highest governance body.

....

G4-37   Report processes for consultation between stakeholders and the highest governance body on economic, environmental and social topics. If consultation is delegated, describe to whom and any feedback processes to the highest governance body.

G4-38   Report the composition of the highest governance body and its committees by:

- Executive or non-executive

- Independence

- Tenure on the governance body

- Number of each individual's other significant positions and commitments, and the nature of the commitments

- Gender

- Membership of under-represented social groups

- Competences relating to economic, environmental and social impacts

- Stakeholder representation

G4-39   Report whether the Chair of the highest governance body is also an executive officer (and, if so, his or her function within the organization's management and the reasons for this arrangement).

G4-40 Report the nomination and selection processes for the highest governance body and its committees, and the criteria used for nominating and selecting highest governance body members, including:

- Whether and how diversity is considered
- Whether and how independence is considered
- Whether and how expertise and experience relating to economic, environmental and social topics are considered
- Whether and how stakeholders (including shareholders) are involved

G4-41 Report processes for the highest governance body to ensure conflicts of interest are avoided and managed. Report whether conflicts of interest are disclosed to stakeholders, including, as a minimum:

- Cross-board membership
- Cross-shareholding with suppliers and other stakeholders
- Existence of controlling shareholder
- Related party disclosures

G4-42 Report the highest governance body's and senior executives' roles in the development, approval, and updating of the organization's purpose, value or mission statements, strategies, policies, and goals related to economic, environmental and social impacts.

G4-43 Report the measures taken to develop and enhance the highest governance body's collective knowledge of economic, environmental and social topics.

G4-44   a. Report the processes for evaluation of the highest governance body's performance with respect to governance of economic, environmental and social topics. Report whether such evaluation is independent or not, and its frequency. Report whether such evaluation is a self-assessment.

b. Report actions taken in response to evaluation of the highest governance body's performance with respect to governance of economic, environmental and social topics, including, as a minimum, changes in membership and organizational practice.

G4-45   a. Report the highest governance body's role in the identification and management of economic, environmental and social impacts, risks, and opportunities. Include the highest governance body's role in the implementation of due diligence processes.

b. Report whether stakeholder consultation is used to support the highest governance body's identification and management of economic, environmental and social impacts, risks and opportunities.

G4-46   Report the highest governance body's role in reviewing the effectiveness of the organization's risk management processes for economic, environmental and social topics.

G4-47   Report the frequency of the highest governance body's review of economic, environmental and social impacts, risks and opportunities.

G4-48 Report the highest committee or position that formally reviews and approves the organization's sustainability report and ensures that all material Aspects are covered.

G4-49 Report the process for communicating critical concerns to the highest governance body.

G4-50 Report the nature and total number of critical concerns that were communicated to the highest governance body and the mechanism(s) used to address and resolve them.

G4-51 Report the remuneration policies for the highest governance body and senior executives for the below types of remuneration:

- Fixed pay and variable pay: performance-based pay
- Equity-based pay
- Bonuses
- Deferred or vested shares
- Sign-on bonuses or recruitment incentive payments
- Termination payments
- Clawbacks
- Retirement benefits, including the difference between benefit schemes and contribution rates for the highest governance body, senior executives and all other employees

Report how performance criteria in the remuneration policy relate to the highest governance body's and senior executives' economic, environmental and social objectives.

G4-52 Report the process for determining remuneration. Report whether remuneration consultants are involved in determining remuneration and whether they are independent of management. Report any other relationships which the remuneration consultants have with the organization.

G4-53 Report how stakeholders' views are sought and taken into account regarding remuneration, including the results of votes on remuneration policies and proposals, if applicable.

G4-54 Report the ratio of the annual total compensation for the organization's highest-paid individual in each country of significant operations to the median annual total compensation for all employees (excluding the highest-paid individual) in the same country.

G4-55 Report the ratio of percentage increase in annual total compensation for the organization's highest-paid individual in each country of significant operations to the median percentage increase in annual total compensation for all employees (excluding the highest-paid individual) in the same country.

As you can see, this is almost a report all on its own. I wonder if this is a knee-jerk reaction to panic following several years of financial crisis and highly visible public debates and stockholder meetings where Board accountability and executive pay became the main topics of the day. I have several reservations about the detail required by these disclosures and wonder if they all add value to our ability, as stakeholders, to assess our relationship with the reporting company and make decisions. Personally, while I agree there is a certain justification to enhance governance and remuneration disclosures in sustainability reporting,

I tend to think that this granularity does not justify the effort to report it. However, companies that consider a COMPREHENSIVE level report to be important, or for which disclosure would represent no significant additional effort, will probably tick all these boxes. Others may question the relevance and prefer to stay at CORE or at an undeclared level. Don't hold me to this, but if there are any revisions of G4 in the pipeline in the coming years, I suspect this will be one of the first sections under review.

ETHICS: Two additional disclosures for COMPREHENSIVE reporters are now part of the G4 General Standard Disclosures. G4-57 and G4-58 require description of *internal and external mechanisms for seeking advice on ethical and lawful behavior, and matters related to organizational integrity, such as helplines or advice lines* and for *reporting concerns about unethical or unlawful behavior, and matters related to organizational integrity, such as escalation through line management, whistleblowing mechanisms or hotlines.* Both these disclosures are new but in general, similar information has tended to be included as part of companies' routine reporting on organizational ethics and Code of Conduct matters.

Key things to note about Disclosures on Management Approach

As mentioned earlier, DMAs now become more important in the context of the need to explain in more detail the company's position on material issues, and, possibly, fewer Performance Indicators being reported. G4 requires a DMA for each Material Aspect reported, although, if the company has identified that several Material Aspects are governed by the same management approach, one DMA will suffice where several may have been required under G3.

G4 has been prescriptive about what a DMA should contain:

a. Report why the Aspect is material. Report the impacts that make this Aspect material.

b. Report how the organization manages the material Aspect or its impacts.

c. Report the evaluation of the management approach, including:

   - *The mechanisms for evaluating the effectiveness of the management approach*

   - *The results of the evaluation of the management approach*

   - *Any related adjustments to the management approach*

In some cases, G4 provides additional guidance (some of which was moved from disclosure content in G3 indicators) to help DMA reporting on specific Aspects. Only a small number of disclosures contain this additional guidance, and you can see which ones in the SSD tables in Figure 6.

Guidance, however, is only guidance and not required to be 'In Accordance'. The real differentiator of G4 reports will be to what extent companies enter into the spirit of reporting rather than the mechanics of reporting. A good DMA will be quite revealing. A minimal DMA will be rather generic and less detailed.

One further point is that in G4 Performance Indicators, as far as possible, tend to require quantitative disclosures. This is different from G3, where there was quite a mix of both qualitative and quantitative disclosures required. In G4, given that performance indicators are selected on the basis of Material Aspects, so the corresponding DMA should contain all the qualitative aspects relating to these Aspects, while the Performance Indicators focus on the quantitative aspects.

Key things to note about Specific Standard Disclosures

Specific Standard Disclosures (SSDs) are, as we now know, determined by the Material Aspects and Topics selected by the reporting company (after due process). In this section, I take a deeper look at the implications and significance of changes to Performance Indicators in the six main GRI indicator categories.

Economic category

The economic category indicators are not significantly different from G3. Changes are generally minor, moving policy elements out of the indicator disclosures (to DMA) and tightening up the language. Note however, G4-EC4 which includes a new reporting requirement to report financial assistance received from governments by country.

Aspect: Economic performance.

- *G4-EC1 Direct economic value generated and distributed.* The second part of G4-EC1 requires reporting of economic value separately at 'country, regional or market level where significant', leaving the company to decide and define significant. This was mostly ignored in G3 reports, but it remains a requirement for G4. It fits with the need to define Material Aspects by location, rather than overall, so this additional element becomes more significant in G4.

- *G4-EC2 Financial implications and other risks and opportunities for the organization's activities due to climate change.* The reporting requirement in G4 includes new detail about the risks and opportunities posed by climate change and the financial implications and costs of management. This is rather an open-ended type of indicator and the skill will be in identifying specific risks in a specific enough way as to be meaningful. Is any business at all immune to the risks of climate change? Quantifying the potential costs of climate change risks opens up rather a sensitive minefield of disclosures which a company may prefer not to make.

- *G4-EC3 Coverage of the organization's defined benefit plan obligations.* This indicator remains the same as its former G3 version (EC3).

Aspect: Market presence.

- *G4-EC4 Financial assistance received from governments.* An interesting detail here requires reporting *by country* of financial assistance received from the government. For global enterprises, this is a significant addition to the reporting requirement, both from a compilation standpoint and from a disclosure/ transparency perspective – assuming the company does receive assistance from governments around the world as incentives to do business to support economic development. For smaller or local companies, this is not a major change.

- *G4-EC5 Ratios of standard entry level wage by gender compared to local minimum wage at significant locations of operation.* This indicator remains the same as its former G3 version (EC5).

- *G4-EC6 Proportion of senior management hired from the local community at significant locations of operation.* This indicator requires a percentage of senior management hired locally. Locally may mean the local community, region or country and the reporting company must define which. Similarly, senior management may also be defined in different ways. The key thing here is to ensure consistency in reporting over time in a given company.

Aspect: Direct economic impacts.
- *G4-EC7 Development and impact of infrastructure investments and services supported.* This requires a straightforward report of infrastructure investments and impacts. It requires a good understanding of the reporting company on the nature and value of investments in strengthening local communities. Typically, companies have not excelled at calculating such impacts.

- *G4-EC8 Significant indirect economic impacts, including the extent of impacts.* This indicator requires companies to understand their entire value chains and the impacts occurring at different points in the value chain beyond the limits of company operations. The rationale makes sense, but the way this is reported may vary vastly from company to company and the ability of companies to identify and calculate the impact of different business activities is not well developed. Realistically, however, most businesses should know where their impacts are greatest, especially at local level. This aligns well with the requirement to identify Material Aspects where they occur (GSDs G4-21 and G4-21) and identifying impacts on specific communities or locations, rather than broad-scale global impacts, could be a useful and possibly more relevant approach for stakeholders.

Aspect: Procurement practices.

- *G4-EC9 Proportion of spending on local suppliers at significant locations of operation.* As with many G4 indicators, definitions may differ between companies. Does local include purchases from local importers of global manufacturers, or does it relate only to locally manufactured goods? The key is transparency and consistency – disclosing the way this is defined in the reporting company, and measuring consistently over successive reports.

Environment category

The environment category indicators have changed substantially over-all, with six new indicators within the category. Additionally, several indicators have been modified, clarified or combined. The key changes to watch out for include new Scope Three reporting (G4-EN4) and energy and emissions intensity disclosures (G4-EN5 and G4-EN18).

Aspect: Materials.

- *G4-EN1 Materials used by weight or volume*

- *G4-EN2 Percentage of materials used that are recycled input materials*

These indicators remain the same as former G3 indicators (EN1 and EN2).

Aspect: Energy.

- *G4-EN3 Energy consumption within the organization.* The G4 Implementation Manual offers detailed guidance for reporting energy from renewable and non-renewable sources, which typically are understood as Scope 1 and Scope 2 energy sources based on the GHG protocol. G4-EN3 is similar to G3 reporting requirements (although in G3, this was two separate indicators for direct and indirect energy, EN3 and EN4). This now ensures a clearer picture of the total energy consumption of a company.

• *G4-EN4 Energy consumption outside of the organization.* This is a new disclosure, and detailed guidance is provided in the G4 Implementation Manual. The indicator covers Scope 3 energy sources, which many companies have yet to determine. For COMPREHENSIVE reporters that note Energy as a Material Aspect, this could be a deal-breaker. The challenges of identifying Scope 3 energy consumption are not insignificant, while some may be easier, especially in complex supply chains.

• *G4-EN5 Energy intensity.* This is a new indicator and is designed to offer a way for companies to present energy consumption in context. Companies have a wide berth to define this context, against which energy is normalized using a constant variable, which counters the effect of business changes and offers a small degree of comparability with other organizations, if the same normalization factor is used. GRI offers three normalization factors: product intensity (such as energy consumed per unit produced); service intensity (such as energy consumed per function or per service); and sales intensity (such as energy consumed per monetary unit of sales). However, companies can select whatever makes most sense to them: for example, per meter squared of factory or office space is often used in certain sectors. The good thing about the intensity measurement is that it gives a sense of underlying data trends, and, if normalized to a controllable variable such as per product unit, offers clues to the organization about how to manage energy more efficiently. The downside is that energy intensity is often presented as a major achievement, when in fact companies are using ever-increasing absolute volumes of energy, which is not sustainable. In reality, we need to see both absolute and intensity data to understand a company's impacts and sustainability management. With COMPREHENSIVE reporters, this will be possible if Energy is a Material Aspect. With CORE reporters, who are required to report one energy indicator if energy is a Material Aspect, selection of the intensity measure may give an inaccurate overall picture.

- *G4-EN6 Reduction of energy consumption.* G4-EN6 combines two former G3 indicators (EN5 and EN7), but otherwise no significant change.

- *G4-EN7 Reductions in energy requirements of products and services.* This indicator remains the same as its former G3 version (EN6).

Aspect: Water.
- *G4-EN8 Total water withdrawal by source*

- *G4-EN9 Water sources significantly affected by withdrawal of water*

- *G4-EN10 Percentage and total volume of water recycled and reused*

These indicators remain largely the same as former G3 indicators (EN8, EN9, EN10).

Aspect: Biodiversity.
- *G4-EN11 Operational sites owned, leased, managed in, or adjacent to, protected areas and areas of high biodiversity value outside protected areas*

- *G4-EN12 Description of significant impacts of activities, products, and services on biodiversity in protected areas and areas of high biodiversity value outside protected areas*

- *G4-EN13 Habitats protected or restored*

- *G4-EN14 Total number of IUCN Red List species and national conservation list species with habitats in areas affected by operations, by level of extinction risk*

These indicators remain largely the same as former G3 indicators (EN11, EN12, EN13, EN14, EN15) though they have been reordered and somewhat simplified, and reduced from five indicators to four.

Aspect: Emissions.
- *G4-EN15 Direct greenhouse gas (GHG) emissions (Scope 1)*

- *G4-EN16 Energy indirect greenhouse gas (GHG) emissions (Scope 2)*

- *G4-EN17 Other indirect greenhouse gas (GHG) emissions (Scope 3)*

- *G4-EN18 Greenhouse gas (GHG) emissions intensity*

- *G4-EN19 Reduction of greenhouse gas (GHG) emissions*

- *G4-EN20 Emissions of ozone-depleting substances (ODS)*

- *G4-EN21 NOX, SOX, and other significant air emissions*

Emissions indicators have been reordered in the same way as the energy aspect indicators and the same implications of the changes apply here. Emissions reporting now aligns more closely with the Greenhouse Gas Protocol, and a new indicator for Emissions Intensity (G4-EN18) is included.

Aspect: Effluents and waste.

- *G4-EN22 Total water discharge by quality and destination*

- *G4-EN23 Total weight of waste by type and disposal method*

- *G4-EN24 Total number and volume of significant spills*

- *G4-EN25 Weight of transported, imported, exported, or treated waste deemed hazardous under the terms of the Basel Convention Annex I, II, III, and VIII, and percentage of transported waste shipped internationally*

- *G4-EN26 Identity, size, protected status, and biodiversity value of water bodies and related habitats significantly affected by the organization's discharges of water and runoff*

These indicators remain largely the same as former G3 indicators (EN21–EN25).

Aspect: Products and services.

- *G4-EN27 Extent of impact mitigation of environmental impacts of products and services*

- *G4-EN28 Percentage of products sold and their packaging materials that are reclaimed by category*

These indicators remain largely the same as former G3 indicators (EN26–EN27); however, in order to avoid overlap with other SSDs, the specific compilation of G4-EN27 excludes a requirement to report detailed impacts by type and offers this as guidance only.

Aspect: Compliance.
- *G4-EN29 Monetary value of significant fines and total number of non-monetary sanctions for non-compliance with environmental laws and regulations*

This indicator remains largely the same as former G3 indicator EN28.

Aspect: Transport.
- *G4-EN30 Significant environmental impacts of transporting products and other goods and materials for the organization's operations, and transporting members of the workforce*

This indicator remains largely the same as former G3 indicator EN29.

Aspect: Overall.
- *G4-EN31 Total environmental protection expenditures and invest-ments by type*

This indicator remains largely the same as former G3 indicator EN30.

Aspect: Supplier environmental assessment.
- *G4-EN32 Percentage of new suppliers that were screened using environmental criteria*

- *G4-EN33 Significant actual and potential negative environmental impacts in the supply chain and actions taken*

This is the first time we meet an entirely new category of indicators which show up four times in the separate reporting categories: Environment, Human rights, Labor practices and Society, and together, are designed to ensure a much stronger presence of supply chain impacts in any G4 report, where supply chain impacts are material for an organization. This set of indicators relating to supplier screening and negative impacts are identical in terms of reporting requirements in each of the disclosure categories. Remember that the Material Aspect Boundary may now be specific to a country, a type of operation or a certain market segment, so disclosure may be limited to parts of the supply chain and not the entire operation.

In any event, these new indicators require detailed disclosure of the application of screening of new suppliers for different aspects of ethical and responsible behavior relative to the specific reporting category and the negative or potentially negative impacts generated and the way in which these have been addressed. The reporting requirements include the disclosure of how improvements have been applied and how many suppliers were terminated for non-adherence to required principles and practices.

In general, this disclosure, as it applies in all categories, requires companies to apply, monitor and track great detail about their supply chains. For those companies for which aspects of the supply chain are material and that have reported before, it's probably true that they have already disclosed much of this data and these new disclosures may not present significant additional elements. For new reporters for whom this is a Material Aspect, this raises the bar for minimal supply chain disclosure. This is generally regarded as a positive step, given the increasing complexity of global supply chains and the increasing frequency with which we continue to hear about supply chain deficiencies and problems arising through inadequate outsourced supplier practices.

Aspect: Environmental grievance mechanisms.

- *G4-EN34 Number of grievances about environmental impacts filed, addressed, and resolved through formal grievance mechanisms.*

Similar to the new Supplier Assessment Aspect indicators G4-EN32 and G4-EN33, this disclosure is repeated four times in the separate reporting categories: Environment, Human rights, Labor practices and Society, and together are designed to ensure the much stronger presence of supply chain management aspects in all the activities of companies. This indicator is strongly influenced by the United Nations (UN) 'Guiding Principles on Business and Human Rights, Implementing the United Nations "Protect, Respect and Remedy" Framework', 2011 and includes disclosure of the existence of formal grievance mechanisms as well as the grievances that have been filed and resolved. For both existing and new reporters, where this is considered a Material Aspect, this type of disclosure may be a little sensitive. Formal grievance mechanisms are defined as 'systems consisting of specified procedures, roles and rules for methodically addressing complaints as well as resolving disputes. Formal grievance mechanisms are expected to be legitimate, accessible, predictable, equitable, rights-compatible, clear and transparent, and based on dialogue and mediation' (G4IM, p. 248).

Social category: Labor practices and decent work

Labor practices indicators remain largely the same, with three exceptions. Two labor indicators relating to employee numbers and employee participation in Collective Bargaining Agreements have moved to General Standard Disclosures, and must be reported by all companies. The second change relates to the addition of G4-LA14, G4-LA15 and G4-LA16, new indicators found in several categories which bolster labor practices and human rights disclosures in the supply chain. The third change relates to G4-LA3, which was one of the additional labor rights clauses in G3.1

Aspect: Employment.

- *G4-LA1 Total number and rates of new employee hires and employee turnover by age group, gender, and region*

- *G4-LA2 Benefits provided to full-time employees that are not provided to temporary or part-time employees, by significant locations of operation*

- *G4-LA3 Return to work and retention rates after parental leave, by gender*

These indicators remain largely the same as former G3 indicators: EN21–EN25.

Aspect: Labor/management relations.

- *G4-LA4 Minimum notice periods regarding operational changes, including whether these are specified in collective agreements.* This indicator remains largely the same as former G3 indicator LA5.

Aspect: Occupational health and safety.

- *G4-LA5 Percentage of total workforce represented in formal joint management–worker health and safety committees that help monitor and advise on occupational health and safety programs*

- *G4-LA6 Type of injury and rates of injury, occupational diseases, lost days, and absenteeism, and total number of work-related fatalities, by region and by gender*

- *G4-LA7 Workers with high incidence or high risk of diseases related to their occupation*

- *G4-LA8 Health and safety topics covered in formal agreements with trade unions*

These indicators remain largely the same as former G3 indicators: LA6, LA7 and LA9. Note that in G4-LA7, the requirement is to report the number of employees with high incidence or risk of disease and not, as in the former disclosure LA8 which was similar, to also report education and training to assist workforce members, their families or community members regarding serious diseases. I consider G4-LA7 to be a new indicator rather than a simple modification as it places prime emphasis on describing actual risk in the business rather than activities designed to educate and prevent.

Aspect: Training and education.

- *G4-LA9 Average hours of training per year per employee by gender, and by employee category*

- *G4-LA10 Programs for skills management and lifelong learning that support the continued employability of employees and assist them in managing career endings*

- *G4-LA11 Percentage of employees receiving regular performance and career development reviews, by gender and by employee category*

These indicators remain largely the same as former G3 indicators: LA10, LA11 and LA12.

Aspect: Diversity and equal opportunity.

- *G4-LA12 Composition of governance bodies and breakdown of employees per employee category according to gender, age group, minority group membership, and other indicators of diversity*

This indicator remains largely the same as former G3 indicator LA13.

Aspect: Equal remuneration for women and men.

- *G4-LA13 Ratio of basic salary and remuneration of women to men by employee category, by significant locations of operation.* This indicator remains largely the same as former G3 indicator LA14.

Aspect: Supplier assessment for labor practices.

- *G4-LA14 Percentage of new suppliers that were screened using labor practices criteria*

- *G4-LA15 Significant actual and potential negative impacts for labor practices in the supply chain and actions taken*

See explanation in Environment category: G4 EN32-33.

Aspect: Labor practices grievance mechanisms.

- *G4-LA16 Number of grievances about labor practices filed, addressed, and resolved through formal grievance mechanisms*

See explanation in Environment category: G4 EN-34.

Social category: Human rights

Human rights indicators have been both upgraded in G4, including former G3.1 indicators, adding in one new indicator regarding negative impacts relating to human rights in the supply chain and also, integrating human rights indicators in three other categories. See the section on Environmental category disclosures above for a more detailed explanation of this. This follows the increasing focus on human rights, especially in complex and outsourced supply chains which have been regularly in the news in recent years, whether this relates to fires in factories in the Far East, suicides, forced labor in Eastern Europe or other high-exposure incidents which have the potential to seriously damage business reputation, as well as business continuity.

Aspect: Investment.

- *G4-HR1 Total number and percentage of significant investment agreements and contracts that include human rights clauses or that underwent human rights screening*

- *G4-HR2 Total hours of employee training on human rights policies or procedures concerning aspects of human rights that are relevant to operations, including the percentage of employees trained*

These indicators remain largely the same as former G3 indicators: HR1 and HR3.

Aspect: Non-discrimination.

- *G4-HR3 Total number of incidents of discrimination and corrective actions taken*

Aspect: Freedom of association and collective bargaining.

- *G4-HR4 Operations and suppliers identified in which the right to exercise freedom of association and collective bargaining may be violated or at significant risk, and measures taken to support these rights*

Aspect: Child labor.

- *G4-HR5 Operations and suppliers identified as having significant risk for incidents of child labor, and measures taken to contribute to the effective abolition of child labor*

Aspect: Forced or compulsory labor.

- *G4-HR6 Operations and suppliers identified as having significant risk for incidents of forced or compulsory labor, and measures to contribute to the elimination of all forms of forced or compulsory labor*

Aspect: Security practices.

- *G4-HR7 Percentage of security personnel trained in the organization's human rights policies or procedures that are relevant to operations*

Aspect: Indigenous rights.

- *G4-HR8 Total number of incidents of violations involving rights of indigenous peoples and actions taken*

Aspect: Assessment.

- *G4-HR9 Total number and percentage of operations that have been subject to human rights reviews or impact assessments*

All the above indicators G4-GR3 through G4-HR9 remain largely unchanged and correspond to former G3 indicators HR4 through HR10, in the same order. Where there are changes, these are minor and mainly refer to the degree of guidance provided versus specific disclosure requirements.

Aspect: Supplier human rights assessment.

- *G4-HR10 Percentage of new suppliers that were screened using human rights criteria*

- *G4-HR11 Significant actual and potential negative human rights impacts in the supply chain and actions taken*

See explanation in Environment category: G4 EN32-33. G4-HR10 was included in G3 (HR2).

Aspect: Human rights grievance mechanisms.
- *G4-HR12 Number of grievances about human rights impacts filed, addressed, and resolved through formal grievance mechanisms*

This indicator remains largely the same as former G3 indicator HR11.

Social category: Society

This category includes the addition of G4-SO9, G4-SO10 and G4 SO-11, new indicators found in several categories which bolster supply chain and human rights disclosures. Former G3 disclosure SO5 and SO10 have been removed and added into the reporting guidance in Public Policy Aspect DMA and G4-SO2, respectively.

Aspect: Local communities.
- *G4-SO1 Percentage of operations with implemented local community engagement, impact assessments, and development programs*

- *G4-SO2 Operations with significant actual or potential negative impacts on local communities*

These indicators remain largely the same as former G3 indicators: SO1 and SO9. G4-SO2 includes guidance from former G3 indicator SO10.

Aspect: Anti-corruption.
- *G4-SO3 Total number and percentage of operations assessed for risks related to corruption and the significant risks identified*

- *G4-SO4 Communication and training on anti-corruption policies and procedures*

- *G4-SO5 Confirmed incidents of corruption and actions taken*

These indicators remain largely the same as former G3 indicators: SO2, SO3 and SO4.

Aspect: Public policy.
- *G4-SO6 Total value of political contributions by country and recipient/beneficiary*

This indicator remains largely the same as former G3 indicator SO6 and includes guidance from former G3 indicator SO5.

Aspect: Anti-competitive behavior.
- *G4-SO7 Total number of legal actions for anti-competitive behavior, anti-trust, and monopoly practices and their outcomes*

Aspect: Compliance.
- *G4-SO8 Monetary value of significant fines and total number of non-monetary sanctions for non-compliance with laws and regulations*

These indicators remain largely the same as former G3 indicators: SO7 and SO8.

Aspect: Supplier assessment for impacts on society.
- *G4-SO9 Percentage of new suppliers that were screened using criteria for impacts on society*

- *G4-SO10 Significant actual and potential negative impacts on society in the supply chain and actions taken*

See explanation in Environment category: G4 EN32-33.

Aspect: Grievance mechanisms for impacts on society.

- *G4-SO11 Number of grievances about impacts on society filed, addressed, and resolved through formal grievance mechanisms*

See explanation in Environment category: G4-EN34.

Social category: Product responsibility

This category has the fewest changes in G4, and even eases the disclosure burden in some cases, making reporting a little easier on the reporting companies. No new disclosures have been added.

Aspect: Customer health and safety.

- *G4-PR1 Percentage of significant product and service categories for which health and safety impacts are assessed for improvement*

- *G4-PR2 Total number of incidents of non-compliance with regulations and voluntary codes concerning the health and safety impacts of products and services during their life cycle, by type of outcomes*

G4-PR1 is now easier to report, with the detailed reference to life-cycle states of product development removed and leaving a general percentage of life-cycle assessments to be reported.

Aspect: Product and service labeling.

- *G4-PR3 Type of product and service information required by the organization's procedures for product and service information and labeling, and percentage of significant product and service categories subject to such information requirements*

- *G4-PR4 Total number of incidents of non-compliance with regulations and voluntary codes concerning product and service information and labeling, by type of outcomes*

- *G4-PR5 Results of surveys measuring customer satisfaction*

These indicators remain largely the same as former G3 indicators: PR3 and PR4. In G4-PR5, aspects relating to customer survey practices (which should be disclosed in DMA if this is Material) have been reported from the disclosure requirement as part of the performance indicator.

Aspect: Marketing communications.
- *G4-PR6 Sale of banned or disputed products*

- *G4-PR7 Total number of incidents of non-compliance with regulations and voluntary codes concerning marketing communications, including advertising, promotion, and sponsorship, by type of outcomes*

Aspect: Customer privacy.
- *G4-PR8: Total number of substantiated complaints regarding breaches of customer privacy and losses of customer data*

Aspect: Compliance.
- *G4-PR9 Monetary value of significant fines for non-compliance with laws and regulations concerning the provision and use of products and services*

These indicators remain largely the same as former G3 indicators: PR6, PR7, PR8 and PR9. In G4-PR6, the disclosure content has been reduced to a quantitative response with approaches and procedures moving to DMA reporting.

Key things to note about
Sector Supplements

Sector Supplements that are in final version format and were required for use with G3 Application Level A Reports and are now required at G4 COMPREHENSIVE level, are in the process of being converted to the G4 format, though the content does not change.

At the time of writing, there are ten Sector Supplements in final version, available on the GRI website:

- Airport operators

- Construction and real estate

- Electric utilities

- Event organizers

- Financial services

- Food processing

- Media

- Mining and metals

- NGO

- Oil and gas

A few more are available in pilot version.

At present, two supplements, Financial Services Sector and Mining and Metals Sector, have been converted to the G4 format, and include additional sector-specific Specific Standard Disclosures in existing G4

Aspects, and in some cases, adding new Aspects. However, as with the overall approach in G4, the sector specific disclosures are required to be reported 'only if the G4 Aspect is considered material by the organization'. Therefore, reporters who wish to be 'In Accordance' with G4, must use the relevant Sector Supplement, if one exists, and respond to all the SSDs which are part of a selected Material Aspect, whether generic or sector specific.

I believe GRI would benefit from making Sector Supplements a priority for future development, together with much more extensive work on Material Aspects by sector. This looks as if it has been low-key for GRI, with only ten such supplements available to date, including NGO and Event organizer supplements, important though they may be, hardly the top priorities in corporate reporting to date. Given that G4 now makes overall comparability virtually impossible, and that there is increasing focus on sectors and the specific impacts they should be accountable for, I believe improved and more extensive sector focus will be a priority. This would not only enable G4 to become much more relevant for a wider range of companies, it would also enable GRI to develop a network of relations with the multitude of sector organizations that are starting to lead sustainability initiatives in their sectors. This could significantly strengthen GRI and add momentum to the G4 uptake.

It looks like the GRI has been overtaken in this initiative by the newly formed Sustainability Accounting Standards Board – SASB – which has an objective '*to provide standards for use by publicly-listed corporations in the U.S. in disclosing material sustainability issues for the benefit of investors and the public. SASB standards are designed for disclosure in mandatory filings to the Securities and Exchange Commission (SEC), such* *as the Form 10-K and 20-F. SASB standards will result in the improved performance of 13,000+ corporations, representing over $16 trillion in funds, on the highest-priority environmental, social and governance issues'* (**www.sasb.org**). SASB is working to an ambitious timeline that envisages production of standards in ten broad sectors by 2014:

- Health care

- Financials

- Technology & communication

- Non-renewable resources

- Transportation

- Services

- Resource transformation

- Consumption

- Renewable resources & alternative energy

- Infrastructure

SASB was born to fill a gap in the sustainability reporting landscape relating to materiality. Most sustainability reports to date have not treated this seriously enough, and this has been underplayed in GRI Frameworks to date. Now that G4 makes materiality center-stage, SASB standards will become a very interesting and helpful tool for companies in their materiality process and prioritization. Despite the fact that SASB's focus is US publicly listed companies, the sector materiality conclusions will be relevant for a much wider group of companies around the world.

What should you do?

While preparing your G4 report, keep an eye on SASB and use relevant sector guidance as it becomes available as input to your materiality process. Use your materiality process to engage stakeholders and gain immeasurable value by understanding what's important to them, and how this aligns with your business strategy. Make materiality work to import your business and your impacts.

....

CHAPTER 7

Will G4 Mean No More Reporting to Other Frameworks?

Key things to note about harmonization

ONE OF THE BIG OBJECTIVES for G4 was harmonization with other reporting frameworks, so that companies would be able to report once, using the G4 Framework, and this would cover all their bases for reporting against other required frameworks. This is a pipedream if ever there was one. Reporting frameworks and individual initiatives are mushrooming beyond anyone's expectations, and while there is some common ground, there is no harmonization, no consistency of formats or submission requirements and no alignment among data users. Forget harmonization. It won't happen in our lifetime. Companies need to make a selection from the various data-demanders and decide which data they will report, to whom, how and when. A G4 report may cover some of this, but it will by no means suffice as your sole sustainability disclosure.

G4 has done us the favor of noting references used in the preparation of G4 guidelines and identified reporting overlap with the UN Global Compact principles, the OECD Guidelines for Multinational Enterprises and the UN Guiding Principles on Business and Human Rights. This is of

limited help. For example, the UNGC Communication on Progress (http://
unglobalcompact.org/COP/communicating_progress/cop_policy/
cop_levels.html) now differentiates between four levels (Learner, Active,
Advanced and LEAD), each of which require specific disclosures against
certain aspects of the UNGC Ten Principles. However, no detail or
alignment is provided, simply a general reference that a certain principle
correlates with a certain disclosure. No correlation is provided to the CEO
Water Mandate required disclosures. There is also no such correlation
to the Carbon Disclosure Project (CDP). The UNGC COP and the CDP
are the most prevalent frameworks that companies use in addition to
sustainability reporting.

Bottom line

Forget harmonization. Go instead for prioritization and selection.

Key things to note about integration

Another originally stated objective of G4 was to align with the Integrated
Reporting framework currently under development by the International
Integrated Reporting Council (IIRC). This was not achieved, largely I
believe because the interests of the IIRC and GRI are diametrically
opposed, despite the hype to the contrary. Integrated Reporting is a
framework that is designed to serve the financial community, so that
they, and the companies they show interest in, can make more money.
Sustainability reporting is inherently designed to provide information to all
stakeholders, and, arguably, especially those who are not shareholders
or have a specific financial interest. Of course, it is difficult to draw the
line between non-financial and financial interests. Even an unskilled

plant operator with a pension plan has a vested interest in the financial success of the pension fund investments, to secure her or his future. The question is one of emphasis. The IIRC has a financial focus with an incorporation of sustainability impacts, insofar as they affect the way a company creates (financial) value. Sustainability reporting expresses accountability for the impacts of a company on people and planet, of which many can be quantified into financial terms, such as climate change risks and emissions management. So while an Integrated Report should demonstrate sustainable thinking, and a sustainability report should demonstrate integrated thinking, these two reporting modes are different and should, in my view, remain separate. Even the CEO of the GRI, Ernst Ligteringen, repeated many times at the GRI Conference in Amsterdam in May 2013, that 'In order to produce and integrated report, you have to have something to integrate!'

Bottom line

Don't look to G4 to help you with integrated reporting, just with better sustainability reporting, which may ultimately be part of your integrated reporting efforts.

CHAPTER 8

Does My G4 Report Need to be Audited?

Key things to note about assurance

G4 DOES LITTLE TO ELEVATE the status of assurance or clarify the cloud of fuzziness that surrounds what I call the Wild West of sustainability reporting assurance. A G4 report, CORE or COMPREHENSIVE, does not require external assurance in order to be 'In Accordance'. G4 brings two changes on the matter of assurance.

First, G4-33 now includes a requirement, for those companies including an assurance statement, to report the relationship between the organization and the assurance providers and to report whether the highest governance body or senior executives are involved in seeking assurance for the sustainability report. This doesn't add much.

Second, G4 is a little more helpful because it now requires a company to identify, as part of the GRI Index, exactly which disclosures, both GSDs and SSDs, have been externally assured individually. This means you won't have to spend hours trying to interpret the assurance statement to work out exactly what it refers to. It also means that reporters will not be able to claim the 'report' is assured when in reality only a small part of the content has been externally reviewed, such as carbon emissions.

At this point, it is not clear just how assurance will work for G4. How will a company assure GSD G4-18 (explain the process for defining report content and how the company has applied the reporting content principles) and G4-19 (list all the Material Aspects identified in the process for defining report content)? Does the assurance refer to the existence of a process, the quality of the process or whether the conclusions of the process are logical outputs of the process, or even, logical in the context of the reporting company? How will assurance providers define the service they offer to reporting companies in this area and how will companies present assurance in their reports?

I believe that sustainability reports should be audited, just as financial reports are professionally audited. I think assurance should be split into two parts:

- *First, audit the data that is presented.* The quantitative data in the report should be audited, not 'assured', so that first and foremost, stakeholders can know the data is correct and an audit trail is available to prove it. Equally, the audit should include a check of whether application of the G4 framework meets the requirements of an 'In Accordance' report, so that stakeholders can know that if a disclosure is claimed, it also exists. Typically, this type of audit would need to be conducted by auditing professionals who have the necessary expertise in auditing methods and processes.

- *Second, assure the selection of information that is presented.* Typically, this will refer to the more qualitative aspects – the judgments, interpretations and narratives and the degree to which they are representative, inclusive and balanced in the broader context of the environment in which the company does business. Does the list of Material Aspects actually make sense? Can a company in the alcohol sector not reasonably include an issue relating to responsible drinking as a Material Topic? Has the reporting company actually disclosed the truly important issues, or have thorny subjects been conveniently left out? A qualitative assurance of a sustainability report will require prior knowledge of the company, the sector, relevant current affairs and significant sustainability issues in locations in which the company operates. Often, these perspectives are best gained by a group of professionals or relevant experts who are brought together in the form of a Stakeholder Panel or Report Advisory Committee, possibly spanning different countries for a global company and different areas of expertise.

G4 could have been an opportunity to move away from the unsatisfactory current reality of assurance to a crisper and more refreshing approach to auditing and assurance which would give report users greater confidence that sustainability reports are professional, quality documents which companies are committed to and are prepared to have submitted to detailed scrutiny. If we cannot trust sustainability reports, their value in helping create our sustainable future is limited.

As an aside, generally speaking, companies that undertake rigorous assurance find that the process adds value internally. Assurers will often provide a private report to a company, which lists detailed recommendations for improving the robustness of data collection processes, balance and quality of information and perspectives on materiality. Irrespective of what gets published, such a process can add great value to sustainability management.

'The changes of the new *G4 Framework* have been significant, especially in identification and communication of material *ESG* aspects. This is good for organizations trying to develop sustainability reports which are concise and clear, designed to inform stakeholders about environmental, social and governance issues which are of interest to them.' ALBERTO GUAJARDO, CAPACITARSE

CHAPTER 9

Additional Insights for Reporters and Non-reporters

For reporters

THE G4 FRAMEWORK, as did its predecessors, applies to all companies of all shapes and sizes anywhere in the world. The graduated Application Level approach offered smaller companies or first-timers a way in, and an opportunity to brand themselves as sustainability-oriented without over-stretching, while also offering companies a path to demonstrate improvement. Companies who start out at G4 COMPREHENSIVE level do not now have a natural route to demonstrate continuous improvement in their reporting (not only their performance), because there is no COMPREHENSIVE PLUS, or higher. Yet.

At the time of writing, the GRI Reports Database showed 1,895 reports were published in 2012 and declared an A, B or C Application Level (with or without external assurance). This represents 61% of the 3,074 reports in the database for that year (which we know is probably no more than half of the actual number of reports published). Of these 1,895 reports, the split between A, B and C is surprisingly equal in percentage terms:

GRI Database, 2012 reports by Application Level	
A	35%
B	38%
C	26%

A level reporters will, in all probability, be reluctant to report at CORE level as this may feel a little like they are going backwards. C level reporters probably have no compelling reason to strive for COMPREHENSIVE unless their stakeholders specifically request it. This leaves B level reporters with the dilemma of going up or going down. In my view, the vast majority will report at CORE level, at least for a few reporting cycles, as this makes most sense and is certainly a respectable choice.

Probably the question of which way to jump is not that significant. The real question is how reporters will use the flexibility and possibilities of the new G4 Framework with integrity, wisdom and a genuine level of sustainability and transparency maturity. If they do, then the most core of CORE reports are likely to be higher quality than some of the best of the Application Level A reports. This is really what G4 is all about – not just improving relevant transparency, but enhancing the accountability and ownership for reporting, and therefore, as an outcome, the quality.

SME reporters and first time reporters should find G4 CORE a reasonable framework and entry into sustainability reporting. I don't think an SME-G4 version is necessary, though others disagree. The smaller and simpler the business, the fewer the hard-hitting material issues, and the more compact the report becomes. However, even small companies or first-time reporters must get with the G4 mindset and not set out to tick-box, as this is self-defeating. First, strategy and process, then action, then report, if you want to be 'In Accordance'. Having said that, SMEs and first-timers that cannot stretch to meet G4 CORE requirements should not delay their reporting journey. Even a non-GRI report, and there are many excellent ones around, is a worthwhile endeavor and should not be dismissed.

For non-reporters

Report-users. Most of this book has focused on how to understand and navigate G4 in order to write reports. However, reports are also used by a wide range of stakeholders and G4 presents a new opportunity for these stakeholders to understand reporting in a different way and engage with companies at a higher level. Just as the G4 mind-set for reporters moves away from and indicator-driven approach toward a process-driven approach, so the G4 report-user should look for deep evidence of application of the reporting principles, process, dialog and appropriate selection of material issues.

Sustainability reporting is not a competition, although it does have competitive value. With G4, the symbolic 'A+' has been taken away from reporters, and reporting companies now have to adjust to a more mature reporting approach where the value is in the doing as much as in the publishing. Report-users need to understand this. We need to be less quick to jump to the conclusion that a COMPREHENSIVE reporter is 'better' than a CORE reporter. We need to avoid counting material issues and judging companies more favorably if there are more issues rather than fewer. G4 report-users must accept that there will be wide variations in G4 reports, and that each one should be assessed on its own merits, and not simply because there are more tables and charts.

As a report user, when opening a G4 report, I will first look at the five powerful anchoring General Standard Disclosures: G4-17–G4-21. The quality of response to these disclosures will tell me a great deal about the company and its sustainability and transparency maturity.

Reporting consultants. As a reporting consultant for many years supporting companies in the formulation of their sustainability reports, I believe that G4 offers a much stronger role for CSR or sustainability reporting consultants to be part of the process rather than just part of the report. With G3, it was possible for a company to pile up a whole load of information, dump it on the reporting consultant and expect the consultant to turn it into a GRI-based report, responding to all the GRI disclosures and indicators in order to achieve a certain reporting level. The G3 mindset again, information-centric, not process-centric. Consultants did not have a strong basis to engage with the company beyond collecting information and formulating the report. With G4, the reporting consultant now has a much more compelling argument to engage with the client and help them develop the processes that are required to report in the G4 way. I believe this will help create better relationships between consultants and their clients, and better outcomes in terms of sustainability processes in many companies. I hope so!

CHAPTER 10

The Question on Everybody's Lips: Will G4 Reports be Shorter?

THE ANSWER, OF COURSE, is yes, no and it depends.

The GSDs require quite some load of disclosure, and at COMPREHENSIVE level, far more than the G3 requirement – 58 individual disclosures where G3/G3.1 included only (!) 42 disclosures. Even at CORE level, there are 34 disclosures, where at G3 Application Level C, there were 28 disclosure requirements. The additional disclosure for both levels includes reporting of materiality process and, at COMPREHENSIVE level, governance and remuneration and ethics. Therefore, it's unlikely that the GSD part of any report will be significantly shorter, unless A Level reporters move to CORE reporting.

The SSDs are also no less expansive, but the key here is the selection of Material Aspects and the required level of reporting on DMA for each Aspect, and the number of performance indicators selected based on the CORE or COMPREHENSIVE approach. I suspect that companies who are used to reporting at Application Level A will not significantly cut down their reporting content, and will be eager to include positively oriented information, even though it is not material. Note that G4 does not specify what should NOT be reported, it only established what SHOULD be reported. Also, given G4's limited success at achieving harmonization across different reporting frameworks, companies will want to include in their G4 reports the information that is relevant to other stakeholders, beyond the disclosures required by the G4 Framework.

Bottom line

If anyone is geeky enough to do a study of the length of reports before and after G4, I would place an ice-cream bet that they will not be any shorter.

The real question is, how much longer will they be?

....

Author Perspective:
The G4 Maturity Threshold

BY NOW, YOU HAVE PROBABLY REALIZED that I believe G4 helps us move forward and should be adopted as the universal reporting framework for sustainability reporting. G4 is the product of a long and complex multi-stakeholder process. By its very nature, it contains certain compromises or areas of focus which may not match everyone's expectations or preferences. But it is here, available and ready for use. There is not another framework that helps organize and advance sustainability reporting in the same way. Therefore the issue is not whether G4 is wonderful, but whether G4 users will use it in a wonderful way.

By that, I mean that much more than in the previous reporting framework, G4 requires a mindset change to move from an information-centric to a process–centric approach with materiality at the core. I call this the Maturity Threshold. Companies that manage to use G4 to help drive their own sustainability and transparency maturity will derive significant benefit. Companies that abuse the spirit of G4 by finding loopholes in different disclosure requirements (and there are several loopholes) so as to be able to be minimally transparent while claiming 'In Accordance', are doing themselves a disservice and are unlikely to gain real benefits from the efforts that in any case they have to make to publish a report.

As an eternal optimist, I believe the letter and the spirit of G4 will be a compelling way forward for most companies to cross the Maturity Threshold.

Are you an optimist?

....

For Product Safety Concerns and Information please contact our EU
representative GPSR@taylorandfrancis.com
Taylor & Francis Verlag GmbH, Kaufingerstraße 24, 80331 München, Germany